PRAISE FOR *DATA STORYTELLING IN MARKETING*

T0293184

'Every marketer should include this book in their toolkit to future proof their storytelling skills and maximize the advantage of data-driven marketing.'
Fiona Sweeney, veteran marketer and consultant, Women in Data®

'*Data Storytelling in Marketing* is truly a how-to guide for navigating the complex intersection of data analysis and compelling storytelling. The book shines with its pragmatism, providing a roadmap from the inception to the execution of a great data-based story, laden with examples, real-world case studies, dos and don'ts and insights from industry experts. This approach demystifies data storytelling, making the subject matter accessible and actionable for anyone looking to leverage the power of data in their narratives.'
Julio Franco, Chief Customer Officer, Zappi

'Details how to use the power of data in crafting powerful narratives and stories adapted to your target audiences. Through practical models and case studies, the book demonstrates how insights originating from various datasets can be combined with know-how and sense-making to create differentiation and win in the marketplace.'
Patrick Ubezio, Strategy, Novartis Pharmaceuticals

'If your role involves extracting insight from data, then this book is essential. It offers a masterclass in how to transform data from findings to meaningful insight and persuasive stories. What's more important is that the frameworks shared will help you craft stories that make people pay attention and take action. In a world where data storytelling is becoming more important, this book is a breath of fresh air on how not to rely on bad visualizations that can be interpreted in different ways and to focus on the story that matters in your data.'
Dr Jillian Ney, digital anthropologist and Founder of The Social Intelligence Lab

'Stories have power for humans and can be more powerful with data behind them. This book helps the reader understand how to bring data storytelling to the marketing world, where stories and thoughts are a part of life. Check it out if you are wanting to grow in your marketing abilities.'

Jordan Morrow, Senior Vice President of Data and AI Transformation, AgileOne

'I've found my secret weapon in *Data Storytelling in Marketing*. Caroline Florence's case studies and cheat sheets – packed with insightful and practical dos and don'ts – have become my blueprint for crafting stories that truly resonate. This book is your roadmap to storytelling that engages and persuades.'

Madelaine Oppert, Senior Marketing Manager, iResearch Services

Data Storytelling in Marketing

How to tell persuasive stories through data

Caroline Florence

KoganPage

Publisher's note

Every possible effort has been made to ensure that the information contained in this book is accurate at the time of going to press, and the publishers and author cannot accept responsibility for any errors or omissions, however caused. No responsibility for loss or damage occasioned to any person acting, or refraining from action, as a result of the material in this publication can be accepted by the editor, the publisher or the author.

First published in Great Britain and the United States in 2024 by Kogan Page Limited

Apart from any fair dealing for the purposes of research or private study, or criticism or review, as permitted under the Copyright, Designs and Patents Act 1988, this publication may only be reproduced, stored or transmitted, in any form or by any means, with the prior permission in writing of the publishers, or in the case of reprographic reproduction in accordance with the terms and licences issued by the CLA. Enquiries concerning reproduction outside these terms should be sent to the publishers at the undermentioned addresses:

2nd Floor, 45 Gee Street
London
EC1V 3RS
United Kingdom

8 W 38th Street, Suite 902
New York, NY 10018
USA

www.koganpage.com

Kogan Page books are printed on paper from sustainable forests.

© Caroline Florence, 2024

The right of Caroline Florence to be identified as the author of this work has been asserted by her in accordance with the Copyright, Designs and Patents Act 1988.

ISBNs

Hardback   978 1 3986 1505 2
Paperback   978 1 3986 1503 8
Ebook   978 1 3986 1504 5

British Library Cataloguing-in-Publication Data
A CIP record for this book is available from the British Library.

Library of Congress Cataloging-in-Publication Data
Names: Florence, Caroline, author.
Title: Data storytelling in marketing: how to tell persuasive stories
   through data / Caroline Florence.
Description: London, United Kingdom; New York, NY: Kogan Page, 2024. |
   Includes bibliographical references and index.
Identifiers: LCCN 2024012693 (print) | LCCN 2024012694 (ebook) | ISBN
   9781398615038 (paperback) | ISBN 9781398615052 (hardback) | ISBN
   9781398615052 (ebook)
Subjects: LCSH: Marketing – Data processing. | Customer
   relations–Management–Data processing. | Quantitative research.
Classification: LCC HF5415.125 .F64 2024 (print) | LCC HF5415.125 (ebook)
   | DDC 658.8/340285–dc23/eng/20240402
LC record available at https://lccn.loc.gov/2024012693
LC ebook record available at https://lccn.loc.gov/2024012694

Typeset by Integra Software Services, Pondicherry
Print production managed by Jellyfish
Printed and bound by CPI Group (UK) Ltd, Croydon, CR0 4YY

For my greatest champions – Ryan, Euan and Isaac.
Who never once complained when I said 'I can't right now,
I just need to finish this chapter!'
A huge, big thank you.

CONTENTS

LIST OF FIGURES

ABOUT THE AUTHOR

Caroline Florence is an expert in data analysis, insight generation and creating evidence-based narratives to drive business decisions and actions. Based near Cambridge, UK, she founded the training company Insight Narrator in 2012 and has since worked with over 10,000 individuals to improve their data storytelling. Caroline was included in the Twenty Women in Data and Tech in 2023 for services to learning and development. She was listed in the ESOMAR Insight250 in 2021 as a global innovator in data-driven marketing and she speaks regularly at conferences around the world on the value of insight.

LIST OF CONTRIBUTORS

In developing this book, I have spoken with many experts in marketing and data storytelling and would like to thank the following people for their contribution.

RICHARD COLWELL

Richard is the CEO of Red C Research & Marketing Group, a dynamic, full-service research company based in Ireland, with offices in Dublin and London. Richard is also the Executive Vice President of WIN, the Worldwide Independent Network of Market Research and Opinion Polls, and the Irish Representative of ESOMAR, the global voice of the data, research and insights community.

LUCY DAVISON

Lucy is a communication expert, award-winning keynote speaker, MRS Fellow and ESOMAR UK Rep. The Founder and CEO of Keen as Mustard Marketing, Lucy has over 30 years of experience in B2B marketing, strategy and communications. She has written for the *Independent*, *Marketing*, *Marketing Week* and *Retail Week* and judged the Market Research Awards.

ESTRELLA DÍAZ

Estrella is a leading researcher in the field of smart tourism. She works as a Professor of Marketing at the University of Castilla-La Mancha (UCLM). Estrella has been elected by ESOMAR as one of the 250 pioneering professionals and leading international experts in the field of market research and business intelligence and she is included in the list of the 150 most influential people in tourism in Spain.

GABRIELE ENDERS

Gabriele is Director, Strategic Partnerships Marketing at Boots and No7 Beauty Company. Currently focused on managing agency partnerships to deliver maximum performance, results and efficiencies, Gabriele is an experienced marketing leader with a strong track record across brand management, marketing strategy and operations.

RHEA FOX

Rhea is a customer and digital leader with 20-plus years in strategy, CX, marketing and trading. A growth-obsessed data evangelist and Marketing Week 2022 CX50 winner, Rhea is a regular speaker, contributor, and judge on CX, digital transformation and marketing. Rhea is currently Digital Director at Ted Baker, the British clothing retailer with 500 stores and concessions around the world, and has also worked for brands including Paperchase, Aviva, eBay, GHD and Direct Line Group, as well as RAPP and dmg media.

JACKY GIUDICI

Jacky is Head of Functional and Transformation Capability at Boots and No7 Beauty Company, responsible for sourcing, designing, and delivering flexible global learning solutions to enable teams to operate at their best.

ROSY HARRINGTON

Rosy has worked for the De Beers Group since 2013, having previously worked for Royal Mail and Red Bull. In her most recent role as a Global Brand Planner, Rosy was responsible for informing and driving the global marketing strategy for De Beers consumer brands, inspiring senior management and international marketing teams across China, Hong Kong, India, Japan, the United States, France and the UK with customer insight.

LIZZIE HARRIS

Lizzie is Customer Director at B&Q, the UK's leading home improvement and garden living retailer and part of Kingfisher plc, the international home improvement company, operating 1,400 stores in eight countries across Europe. An experienced marketing analytics professional, Lizzie has also worked for Gymshark, Sainsbury's and Lloyds Banking Group.

JEREMY HOLLOW

Jeremy is the Founder and CEO of Listen + Learn Research, an award-winning agency and the leading global authority on the human side of social data, helping clients tap into the potential of social commerce. A writer for This Social Life, a blog about how people live their lives on social media, and a speaker at SXSW, Jeremy is featured in the ESOMAR Insight250 and Social Intelligence Insider 50.

SINEAD JEFFERIES

Sinead is the SVP of Customer Expertise for Zappi and is a recognized insight industry leader, drawing on 20-plus years' experience, leading teams both client-side and in agencies. She is Chair of the Market Research Society and has previously served as a board member. Sinead is a highly skilled researcher with the ability to cut through findings and have meaningful discussions about driving change and delivering commercial business impact.

RACHAEL KINSELLA

Rachael is Editorial and Content Director at iResearch Services, a global thought leadership, marketing and research agency, specializing in narrative and content creation for B2B clients in professional and financial services, technology, healthcare and energy sectors. Rachael is a CIM-qualified Chartered Marketer, Fellow, MA and CIPR communications professional with 20 years of editorial, communications, full mix marketing and business development experience.

SANICA MENEZES

Sanica is Head of Customer Analytics at Aviva. Featured in the prestigious DataIQ Future Leaders list for 2023 and 2024, she is passionate about maximizing the impact from data to help the business understand its customers and build better, more meaningful products and experiences. Sanica has also held roles at Aimia and Virgin Holidays.

CHARLOTTE NEAL

Charlotte is a senior marketing leader with 20 years' experience in strategy, planning, communications and customer experience. Currently Head of Marketing at Turning Point, a UK social enterprise that supports people with their substance use, mental health or learning disability, she has also held a number of senior marketing roles at Sodexo Health & Care and AXA Health, as well as working as a director in creative and media agencies, including Havas.

REBECCA RUANE

Rebecca is Head of Reader Revenue Insight at *The Guardian*, one of the world's leading English-language newspaper websites, where she is responsible for managing a large team of analysts supporting the business to drive revenue from readers. An experienced insight professional, Rebecca has also worked for Westfield, Aimia, Ticketmaster, JCDecaux and Condé Nast Publications.

RUTH SPENCER

Ruth is an expert in data, insights, loyalty and personalization. She is currently an independent data leadership consultant but has previously held senior positions at Walgreens Boots Alliance, The Co-operative Group and Accenture.

JAKE STEADMAN

Jake is Global Head of Market Research and Data at Canva, the design platform that allows users to create visual materials such as social media posts and presentations. Jake has also held senior insight and marketing roles at Deliveroo, Twitter and O2, is on the main board of the Market Research Society and chairs the MRS Data Analytics Council.

FOREWORD

I have been involved with data, marketing and customer experience for over 30 years, having led advertising, marketing services and customer functions for blue-chip brands such as BT, Royal Mail Group and Dixons, spending nearly two decades at board level growing teams across the world. As a former Chair of the Market Research Society and an ESOMAR Representative, I am passionate about great insight driving customer-centric decision-making and always delivering a return on investment. It never ceases to amaze me, when I work with new organizations, how much intelligence and insight already exists but all too often is siloed or forgotten, and not in the hands of those who could use it to drive change.

As businesses strive to connect with their customers on a deeper level, the ability to harness, interpret and influence with data is critical. It is within this context that the concept of data storytelling emerges as a transformative tool, weaving narratives that not only illuminate insights but also resonate with the human elements of our audience. Effective change most often comes when an insight is transformed into a compelling story that cuts through and captures the imagination. Data storytelling is not merely about presenting information; it is an art form that aligns, connects and transforms data points into a cohesive and persuasive narrative. In a world inundated with information, our ability to tell compelling and memorable stories becomes a strategic differentiator.

I am delighted to introduce this practical guide to data storytelling for marketers, authored by Caroline Florence, an expert trainer and facilitator in creating powerful data stories. As an inaugural winner of Insight250, a worldwide 'who's who' of leaders and pioneers of insight innovations across research, data-driven marketing, insight and business intelligence, Caroline brings a wealth of experience and examples to this book. With an astute understanding of the power inherent in both great data analysis and engaging storytelling, Caroline has crafted a guide that is both enlightening and pragmatic. Tailored to marketers and communication professionals looking to harness the full potential of data storytelling, this book serves as a comprehensive roadmap for both novices and seasoned professionals, guiding you through the intricate process of distilling complex datasets into stories that captivate, resonate and drive action.

From demystifying the technical intricacies of data analysis to providing practical frameworks for constructing narratives and compelling outputs, this book takes you through step by step, using practical examples, case studies, hints and tips, pitfalls to avoid and tried and tested tools and techniques. This book is a must-read for those navigating the complexities of modern marketing.

Embrace the art of data storytelling to create content and experiences that leave a lasting impact on the hearts and minds of your audience – be they customers, peers, stakeholders or decision-makers.

Let the story begin.

Crispin Beale FCA, FMRS, FRSA
Group President, Behaviourally
Senior Strategic Adviser, mTab
Fellow and past Chair, Market Research Society
UK Representative, ESOMAR
CEO, Insight250

PREFACE: MY DATA STORYTELLING JOURNEY

From data cruncher...

My first role in marketing was a university summer job in 1996, working for the UK charity the Royal Society for the Protection of Birds (RSPB), helping them with their Millionth Member campaign. It was my first exposure to using audience and membership data to develop targeted marketing and it gave me the bug for data-led marketing that has stayed with me ever since. Decades on from my first marketing job, the relationship between data and marketing has developed significantly and has been transformative when it comes to targeting, understanding, converting and retaining customers. While my first role involved manually entering data into Microsoft Excel and conducting analysis with pen and paper, marketers nowadays have access to data via a plethora of channels using custom-made dashboards, reporting and knowledge share tools. Accessing, manipulating and using data has been democratized and is no longer the domain of a niche group of specialists.

... through data translator...

My first experience with data storytelling came a year later as part of my recruitment interview for a graduate placement with Kantar, the global marketing services giant. As part of the interview, we were asked to analyse a selection of charts from one of their proprietary advertising measurement tools and then present our interpretation and recommendations to a panel of senior directors. Shortly after my presentation I was called back in to see the directors because they did not agree with my interpretation of one of their brand tracking measures. However, the more I looked at it, the more I was convinced my original interpretation was the correct one. Although the data displayed in the graph was complex, I felt I understood it well enough and that my interpretation, and subsequent recommendations, still stood. But I knew it couldn't be, as they had already told me it was wrong – so I had a dilemma to face. What was I supposed to say to these very experienced researchers given they had already told me I was wrong? I asked them to explain the correct interpretation of the data from the chart. After they had done so, I learnt an invaluable data storytelling lesson – that bad data visualization can lead to poor interpretation. I experienced first-hand how easy it is for people to interpret the same data differently if the story isn't clear, simple and explicit.

... to data storyteller...

Fast forward 12 years from my first job at Kantar to 2010. I had spent all my career working in insight roles within marketing teams in large corporate organizations or marketing planning agencies and I was now working at Royal Mail, the UK postal service, heading up a new and growing marketing analytics function within our wider marketing services team. In this newly formed role, I had been charged with bringing in-house all our analytics relating to communication evaluation, marketing and customer planning, and pricing. The move to bring marketing analytics in-house was driven by a desire to cut external consultant costs and to leverage our own data assets. As the head of the team, my role was to persuade my marketing colleagues to use the new models being created by the team to help make better decisions when marketing to our customers. I learnt very quickly that the fantastic models the team were creating, and the valuable insights we could generate from them, were going to be meaningless if we couldn't tell a persuasive data story to sceptical audiences. Especially if the insights were telling them that we needed to do things differently.

... and business influencer

Sitting on a number of programme boards, where I had to convince senior directors from across brand, marcomms, digital, product, customer services and sales to listen to what the customer was telling us, was a masterclass in the importance of data storytelling in driving change. It became very clear, very quickly, that having valid and insightful data is not enough; it is what you communicate that counts. After one notable meeting where I was sharing performance data, a senior stakeholder commented, 'Just because you have all this data doesn't mean you are right.' Much as it hurt to hear that all the great work the team was creating wasn't valued, it was still one of the most useful pieces of feedback I ever had in my career. It challenged me to think differently about how we use data to tell stories and enabled me to reassess the way we communicated our insights. To be heard we would need to do more than generate credible and actionable insight from the data. We would have to turn that data into compelling, evidence-based stories that the stakeholder audience could not ignore. This experience took me on a quest to find new and different ways to communicate the power of data to inform ideas, strategies and plans. It resulted in a period of experimentation, research and personal development that led me to specialize in helping others develop data storytelling capabilities within their teams. This book is the latest step in the journey.

From practitioner to coach

In 2012 I set up Insight Narrator, a consultancy and training practice, and since then I have worked with thousands of people across multiple sectors to help them not only develop their data stories but also, most importantly, embed a data storytelling mindset, culture and way of working within their business. As a data storytelling trainer and coach, I now know where data storytelling works best, what great data stories are (and are not), what works for different audiences and, most importantly, how to create effective stories that make a difference. The skill is how to find and create these stories efficiently and to weave data storytelling practices into business-as-usual processes.

I have trained people across most continents and those in both centralized and local market roles. I've worked with senior leaders to shift the culture and help them lead from the top, and with interns and recent graduates looking to develop specific storytelling skills. I have coached many hundreds of data storytelling champions across the world, from US retail giants and global CPG, pharmaceutical, automotive, media and financial services brands, to government departments, charities and not-for-profits. I have used data storytelling to internally promote marketing strategy and drive budget decisions, and to develop campaign messages and optimize prospect targeting.

I am now sharing the lessons I have learnt, the tried and tested approaches I have developed, and practical examples gained from working with many different teams, to help you create insightful data stories that influence the hearts and minds of your audience.

ACKNOWLEDGEMENTS

A huge thanks to Crispin Beale, not only for your kind words in the foreword of this book, but for your ongoing mentorship and support over my career.

To all the contributors, some who I have known for decades, some I have worked with more recently, and some I have only met through this book, a huge thank you to you all. I wanted this book to be more than just my perspective on data storytelling for marketing and your perspectives and tips that you shared with me during our conversations make the book infinitely more insightful to the reader.

To the Women in Data crew in general, I thank you for championing the topics that are close to my heart, but to Roisin McCarthy and Fiona Sweeney specifically, an extra special thanks for your help in making this book happen. When I wanted to ensure that my expert contributors included a diverse range of marketing, customer and data professionals, there was only one person to call who has the network and can always make things happen. Roisin, I salute you! And when I wanted someone to be a diligent, but ruthless, beta reader, Fiona was top of my list. The time you have dedicated to giving invaluable feedback is so appreciated and I cannot thank you enough.

Thanks also to Jeylan Ramis and Donna Goddard at Kogan Page for your patience and feedback. Without your input and persistence, it would have been a lot harder to turn the original proposal into a completed manuscript.

To all my clients and colleagues over the years, you have all played a role in shaping my experience and expertise in data storytelling. There are far too many to mention, and I fear I would miss one out, but you know who you are.

And a final thanks to an old boss of mine, who is no longer with us. Janet Hull was a marketing legend and a phenomenal role model.

A tiny, chain-smoking, designer clothes-wearing single mum, who was respected by all for her marketing knowledge, she carved out a role for data storytelling and actionable insight a decade before anyone else was mentioning those terms. Many of the tips in this book started from Janet's mentoring.

v

Introduction

The role of data storytelling as part of the marketing toolkit

In this chapter we will explore:

- the definition of data storytelling

- why data storytelling is a core part of the marketer's toolkit

- how this book can help improve your data storytelling

I can't think of a profession that doesn't require storytelling as a core skill. We're all ultimately selling something, right? Telling good stories is the best way I know of convincing people of what you're selling and taking them on that journey. You can't just deliver data and numbers because it's boring and people won't buy what you're selling. Equally, if you tell a story with no data or evidence people won't buy it. Combining those two things by putting data at the heart of our stories is the best way I know of delivering insight in a way that is memorable and compelling.

Jake Steadman, Global Head of Market Research and Data, Canva

The definition of data storytelling

There are many different definitions of data, insights and data story-telling, so I want to provide my version of each of these, contextualized within the world of marketing and communication, to create a common standardized language throughout the book.

Definition of data

I refer to the word data in its broadest terms, not just as a series of ones and zeros in a computing program. This wider definition focuses on observations, measurements and facts. This might also be referred to as information or evidence. Data, in this context, includes both quantitative and qualitative data.

Types of data used commonly in data storytelling by marketing teams include:

ZERO-PARTY DATA

This is data that has intentionally or proactively been shared with us by audiences, such as:

- responses to polls, surveys or quizzes
- profiling data added to online accounts or loyalty programmes

FIRST-PARTY DATA

This is proprietary data that companies collect directly, with consent, via their own channels. It might include finance data, operational data, customer data or audience data, but typically it captures behaviours. Given it is based on previous or current interactions and transactions with the brand, it is a precious marketing asset. It includes:

- digital interactions (website, apps)
- customer relationship management (CRM) systems
- content engagement
- point of sale systems
- transactions (accounting systems)
- experience interactions with digital support and call centres

For example, typical first-party data sources you might use in marketing include:

- sales performance data for your region, country or category which shows key commercial metrics

- internal marketing data products from CRM systems that provide contact information, purchase history, interaction history, etc., to inform segments and personalization

- purchase data from loyalty cards or payment cards that provide behavioural information

- email marketing data products measuring email open rates, click-through rates and subscriber behaviour that support email campaign optimization

SECOND-PARTY DATA

This is data that businesses haven't collected but is associated with their customers or audiences. This data is gathered by partnering with another organization (through a contractual agreement). It's a very economical way to gather any additional data and ultimately a great way to increase the breadth of understanding we have about our audience that we cannot get from first-party data alone, such as attitudes and needs. For example:

- retail purchase data

- market research, survey data

- data collected as first-party data by channel partners and trusted suppliers in the supply chain that we have a contractual relationship with

Typical second-party data sources you might use in marketing include:

- shopper research from physical stores, which can provide valuable data on in-store customer behaviour and preferences

- market data from suppliers like Kantar, Nielsen, IRI, IGD and Mintel which provides market share and retail purchase information

- customer surveys and market research data, such as brand and communications tracking studies, advertising testing and in-depth customer interviews

- web scraping tools to collect data from websites and forums to gather insights on consumer sentiment, product reviews and competitive intelligence

THIRD-PARTY DATA

This is data collected by a business or other entity that doesn't have any direct link to customers or audiences. It is normally aggregated from several sources and packaged up for sale, including to competitors. From a marketing perspective it can be valuable to support acquisition strategies, but regulation, like the General Data Protection Regulation (GDPR), has reduced marketers' ability to capture and use this as data, as privacy restrictions become tighter and tighter.

Trusted third-party data sources you might use in marketing include:

- social media platforms sharing demographic and behavioural data about users to assist ad evaluation and audience analysis
- external website data, such as Google Analytics, providing insights into website traffic, conversion, content interactions, etc.
- third-party vendors such as Experian, Acxiom and Dun & Bradstreet, which offer vast datasets that can enhance customer profiles, market segmentation and audience targeting
- open source data sources from aggregators or public bodies providing census data on the general population

When we reference data throughout the book, we will be drawing on the definitions above. However, we will assume in most instances it is not the job of the marketing department to transform raw data inputs into clean, consolidated datasets and most of the data you will be drawing on for your data storytelling will come from managed data assets in databases, platforms or portals. These assets are likely to be clean, with some business logic already built in, and in some instances already combine a number of different sources, for example campaign metadata that has been generated from a CRM system, digital campaign performance data from Google Ad Manager, content data from third-party suppliers and unified customer data from first-party sources.

Definition of insight

Although there are many different interpretations of what an insight is, I prefer to go with the perspective shared by Gary Klein in his book *Seeing What Others Don't* (2013). He states that insights are 'an unexpected shift in the way we understand things' but accepts that they can come in several different varieties, rather than there being a one-size-fits-all formula.

In Figure 0.1 I share the Insight Narrator perspective on what constitutes a great actionable insight. While a data observation includes the 'What?', an actionable insight includes:

- What? (the observations from the data)

plus:

- Why? (the link to why it matters)
- So what? (the relevance and relative importance)
- Now what? (the recommended action)

FIGURE 0.1 The definition of an actionable insight

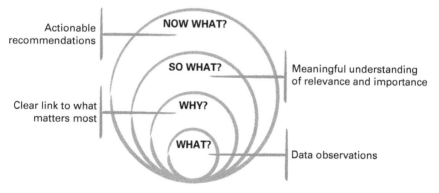

- A data observation is not useful if it doesn't align to 'why' it matters.
- A data observation is not insightful if it doesn't address a clear 'so what' that indicates why this is relevant and important.
- A data observation is a not an actionable if it doesn't lead to a clear 'now what' recommendation that is viable and feasible to activate.

Definition of storytelling

Storytelling in its broadest sense is the writing and telling of stories. Within the context of this book, we are going to focus on business storytelling within marketing and communications teams, rather than this wider definition of storytelling. So, while you may win a prize for fiction or screenwriting in the future, it is unlikely that it is because you have read this book. However, because the audience for a data story is still people and the subject of the data is still people, most of the traditional storytelling techniques still apply. Storytelling is a form of business communication that adapts learnings from wider story structures to persuade audiences to think, to feel and to act.

Definition of data storytelling

When it comes to data storytelling, we focus on how to use storytelling techniques to communicate the insights, actions and ideas that come from the data, rather than the data itself. Therefore, a core part of data storytelling is being able to identify the value of the data available within the broader context of our goals. Then the data storyteller must draw insight out from the background noise, in order to drive the right conclusions and conversations in the story message. What matters is the process to generate sound insights from the vast range of datasets available to the marketing team and how to interpret meaning and sound judgements for decision-making and action taking. Then we can focus on traditional storytelling techniques to bring those insights to life for the audience. These practical skills are where we will focus our attention in this book.

Data reporting is not the same as a data story

As Rutherford David Rogers, Yale Librarian, is quoted as saying in an interview with the *New York Times* (Campbell, 1985), 'we are drowning in information and starving for knowledge'. Using good data in your storytelling is one thing. Doing it well is another. Just having and reporting accurate data is not enough. The problem we have is that, with so much information available, audiences are overloaded. We need to create data stories that share key insights and prioritize evidence that it is crucial to understand, and not just share everything we know.

The sheer wealth of data available risks audiences being paralysed by analysis and not making any decisions until more data is explored. In addition, it can lead to audiences being so confused by what the data is telling them that they default to what they already believe and what they have always done. Both scenarios lead to inertia, conservatism and stagnation.

Data reporting may be preferable as the medium of choice to track measures and key data points required in regular, repeatable outputs. In this instance, analysis, interpretation and insight commentary is either limited to what can be standardized or is automated and generally descriptive with a focus on explaining the data point itself. The rise in platform technology and in the plethora of tools to create dashboards and reports with attractive visuals is a great enabler. But it has led to many leaders believing that if they buy the platform it will give them the insights needed to make accurate and quick decisions. The platform providers have hijacked the term 'data storytelling', making promises that a visualization tool alone just cannot live up to. While good visualization tools can make the data easier to read and process when compared to text or numbers, that alone does not make it a story. And while generative AI provides the potential to automate commentary in reporting, so far it feels generic, one-dimensional and lacking in real insight. As such, there is still a very human role needed to create great data stories.

FIGURE 0.2 The difference between data reporting and data storytelling

Data reporting	Data storytelling
Communicates the data	Communicates the insight and recommendations
Standardized approach	Customized approach
Requires a data-literate audience	Hard work is done for the audience
Relies on good data visualization skills	Relies on good critical and creative thinking skills

Collecting and reporting data is not the same as using data in persuasive storytelling. Figure 0.2 highlights the four key differences between data reporting and data storytelling.

1 Reporting leads with the findings from the data, assuming it will speak for itself. Data storytelling leads with the insights and ideas generated from interpreting the data within the wider commercial context.

2 Reporting is structured to facilitate consistency and standardization. Data storytelling is structured to favour the specific transformation it is designed to evoke. The story itself, and how it is executed, will vary depending on the situation and the need, thus making it harder to standardize and template.

3 Reporting should enable end users to access layers of information, from high-level metrics to detailed sub-analysis. However, this requires a high level of data literacy in the end user and a willingness for them to get their hands dirty. Data storytelling will do the hard work for the end user. Through analysis and interpretation, the data storyteller has generated data-led arguments and will carefully use the data to validate the story.

4 Reporting relies on data visualization to bring the data to life and help the audience navigate through the complexity. Data storytelling

will often use visualization, infographics and interactive reporting tools but it also leverages other storytelling techniques that are mostly absent in reporting. These can be interpretation techniques, such as distillation, inference and judgement, or engagement tools, such as hooks, characters, metaphors and scenarios.

Why data storytelling is a core part of the marketing toolkit

In the ever-evolving landscape of marketing, the effective use of data has become the driving force behind successful brands, activities and campaigns. The rise of digital technologies, martech and the explosion of available data have transformed marketing into a highly data-driven field. Data has emerged as a powerful tool for marketers, providing insights into consumer behaviour, enabling personalized experiences and facilitating evidence-based decision-making. With the advent of social media, digital advertising platforms and CRM systems, the volume and variety of data available to marketers has skyrocketed. From demographic and psychographic information to website analytics and social media engagement metrics, marketers now have access to a wealth of data that can inform their strategies. Given the availability of data, evidence becomes the centrepiece of robust, believable and persuasive marketing stories.

Understanding how to use data to build and tell persuasive stories is an increasingly important part of the modern-day marketer's toolkit and significant progress has been made over the last 10 years. When interviewing the expert contributors for this book, the overwhelming conclusion was that marketing and communication teams have made great strides in data storytelling, including:

- gaining access to better data tools
- upskilling and training teams to improve data literacy
- incorporating data more formally into decision-making
- using data storytelling as part of everyday communications – whether that is with customers, partners or internal teams

Yet, despite the abundance of data and clear progress in data story-telling within marketing and communication functions, many professionals still feel they lack the necessary skills and confidence to effectively analyse and utilize data storytelling techniques to influence others. The data skills gap poses a significant challenge for organizations aiming to harness the power of data-driven marketing. Marketers can lack proficiency and confidence in areas such as data analytics, statistical analysis, data visualization and interpreting insights to drive actionable outcomes. This gap hampers their ability to derive meaningful insights from data to make data-driven decisions, leading to missed opportunities and suboptimal marketing campaigns. Moreover, the inability to effectively communicate data-driven insights to stakeholders can hinder decision-making and undermine trust in the marketing function.

> Data storytelling is something that professional services firms do very well because they've been doing thought leadership for many years, and it's been an integral part of their business development activity. But traditional marketers are often expected just to pick that up from nowhere without any training or opportunity to learn best practice.
>
> **Rachael Kinsella, Editorial and Content Director, iResearch Services**

This book is focused on the data user in the marketing function, rather than the data specialist, and the specific data storytelling skills needed day to day in a marketing or communication role. Over the years that I have worked with marketing strategists and planners, media buyers, campaign managers, brand managers and most other marketing specialists, it is fair to state that the vast majority do buy into the value that data storytelling can offer, but feel they are lacking in time, skills and confidence to do it well. So, whether you are working in digital, brand, internal communication, product management, trade marketing, PR, planning or any other marketing discipline, this book will give you the practical tools to develop stories centred on robust evidence to withstand scrutiny and challenge, provide tangible meaning, offer insight and persuade audiences.

Marketers tend to be natural storytellers who understand the principles of benefit-led messaging and providing audiences with reasons to believe marketing claims, and so will be more comfortable with developing narratives and motivating campaigns than many other business disciplines. They are used to telling stories through their content, but many realize that, in a data-driven world, for these stories to be truly persuasive they need to be evidence-based and clearly communicate the data to the audience. When it comes to being evidence-led in storytelling, many marketers feel a sense of frustration about knowing how to use data storytelling most effectively.

The different data storytelling personas in the marketing department

Within the marketing function, not everyone possesses the same level of data literacy or is starting from the same base when it comes to developing their data storytelling skills. The expert contributors for this book all noted that the data skill sets within marketing functions vary significantly.

> There is a spectrum of data skills in the marketing function. I've seen departments where they just don't use data at all and they do it all on their gut, right through to one of our clients who is so on top of the data. They are not wanting to do lots of data analysis or anything, but they understand the importance of data in terms of driving the marketing plan.
>
> **Richard Colwell, CEO, Red C Research & Marketing Group**

Different individuals exhibit varying degrees of competency and comfort when it comes to working with data, so it makes sense to identify different data storytelling personas within each marketing team. There are four distinct data storyteller personas typically found in different marketing teams. They cover a spectrum from *data sceptics*, who actively avoid using data to inform ideas and decisions if they can, to *data storytelling experts*, who are highly competent in combining data analysis with strong narrative skills to effectively communicate insights and tell compelling stories with data.

As a broad generalization, these four personas represent the varying levels of proficiency and comfort individuals have when working with data to create data stories. While not all marketers or communication professionals need to aspire to expert status, considering where you, or your team, are on the spectrum and what support is required to get to competent is a worthwhile assessment.

THE DATA STORYTELLING SCEPTIC

In the podcast 'Data literacy: The secret to customer obsession' (2020), Jennifer Belissent, Principal Analyst, cites the Forrester Insights-Driven Maturity Model, which found that fewer than 10 per cent of firms are truly insights-driven and more than half of decisions made in businesses are based on gut instinct rather than quantitative information. Within the marketing team there will be sceptics who still resist the idea of using data to inform ideas, evaluate impact and influence others. A sceptic persona may perceive data as both a necessary evil and a threat to their art – one that stifles creativity and natural flair. Sceptics will often see data storytelling primarily as a means to sell-in ideas they already have or decisions already made, rather than seeing data as an asset to inform those ideas and decisions in the first place. They find the complexity and over-measurement of every part of the marketing job unnecessary and a distraction to making solid judgements based on experience and proven marketing theory.

THE ANXIOUS DATA STORYTELLING CONSUMER

The anxious consumer of data stories has limited experience and knowledge of working with data themselves but must use data provided to them as part of their job. They rely on pre-built reports, dashboards or summaries provided by others to make decisions. They lack confidence and feel overwhelmed by data-related tasks and typically rely on others to do the analysis and interpretation so they can then take appropriate actions. They are likely to rely on what they know, the datasets that are provided to them by others, and what sits in their comfort zone, rather than exploring new and different datasets themselves. They may feel anxious about their ability to question, challenge and scrutinize the insights shared with them by others, having to accept them at face value. Potentially curious about generating new insights for themselves, but unsure about collecting the right data and making sense of it to tell a story that stands up to scrutiny, they require some hand-holding to build confidence in experimenting with accessing different sources and support with analysis tasks. This persona typically prefers user-friendly tools that present data in a digestible format, and they do not want to learn the ins and outs of data manipulation, reporting tools or advanced analytics.

Sophie is an experienced marketing manager, having worked in a few different organizations and different marketing disciplines. In her current role she is responsible for developing, managing and optimizing retention campaigns across different business-to-business (B2B) customer touchpoints and channels. She is comfortable with the key metrics used to measure campaign performance and the reports that are generated by the analysts in the team. However, she is also expected to understand customer segment preferences, propensity to churn modelling, loyalty drivers and the role of brand when designing her marketing strategy and plans.

She must influence a number of internal stakeholders across customer experience, sales and service teams to get on board with her plans and ensure that necessary support and resource are in place within the operations. She finds it difficult to convince others proactively with the data and wants to focus more time and energy getting under the skin of customers who are at risk of churning. She would love to be able to tell forward-looking data stories that identify which channels and messages would prevent at-risk customers from leaving but doesn't know where to start.

THE COMPETENT DATA STORYTELLER

The competent data storyteller is proficient in working with data and possesses a solid understanding of data analysis techniques. They are comfortable using tools such as spreadsheets and basic statistical methods to explore data for themselves. They can ask relevant questions, analyse trends and derive insights from data. They are keen to expand their horizons when they have time and are interested in new ways of using data to help them do their role well and influence others. Happy to get their hands dirty with analysis, they can get frustrated with delays and problems accessing data and issues with data imperfection. They can be at risk of potential analysis paralysis without some parameters in which to operate and may often shy away from telling the more complex data stories where the evidence feels ambiguous, lacking in certainty or is contradictory. This persona prefers to be able to effortlessly self-serve and create their own reports, referring to experts only if they hit a problem, they need something explaining in more detail to build their credibility, or they want to utilize more advanced tools. Keen to be at the forefront of what is new, they have an appetite and interest for different technologies, tools and platforms, but possibly don't always know when, why and how these should be used to add value.

James has just graduated with a distinction in his Master's degree in marketing and is working as a Promotions Manager for a publishing company. He works closely with commercial teams internally and with partner brands. Having seen his role become more focused on app-based and digital promotions, he is particularly interested in the use of data to determine optimal targeting, channels and creative, and he found the data analysis part of his Master's programme valuable in building his skills. He works collaboratively with the internal data team when developing the dataset and reporting tools to measure reach, conversion and return on investment (ROI). He would like to find more time to use his data skills to influence the partners and internal stakeholders he works with to prioritize more customized promotions.

THE DATA STORYTELLING EXPERT

The expert is already highly competent in combining data analysis with strong narrative skills to effectively communicate insights and tell compelling stories with data. They can identify meaningful patterns, draw connections across multiple complex sources, align insights with objectives and priorities, as well as craft narratives from the evidence that resonate with their audience. The expert understands the importance of context, audience segmentation and emotional engagement in data storytelling. They use these skills to personalize and tailor their data stories to the different audiences they need to reach and influence. Proactive in spotting new opportunities from insights, they use data storytelling to inspire, sell in strategy, make asks of the wider business and drive change. They are looking to continuously improve their communications and influencing skills, as well as coaching these skills in others.

Amy is an experienced Digital Director with a specific focus on marketing activation. She has a background in customer insight and is familiar with the range of different methods and approaches she can tap into for her data storytelling. Having switched from a research and data role into a digital marketing role she has been able to bring her experience of customer journeys to add rigour to her decision-making. Using her data skills, alongside her leadership and strategic thinking, she has enabled her team to simplify their efforts and processes to focus on the key priorities for both the customer and the business. Seen as a trusted adviser to senior management, she is confident to use evidence to challenge the status quo and she is respected by others for her ability to connect insights to business applicable solutions. Her priority is to empower her wider Digital team to develop their data storytelling skills, so they can improve their broader influence within the business.

Before diving into the detail of this book, reflect on which persona currently resonates with you and where you aspire to be on the data storytelling spectrum. This will help determine the key development areas where you want to drill down into more detail.

How this book can help improve your data storytelling

This book is designed for marketers and communications professionals who want to develop powerful and persuasive stories that transform outcomes. Focused on developing evidence-based storytelling with credible data, this book will help create a paradigm shift in perfor-mance levels within marketing and communications. It is designed to plug the data skills gap and build powerful capabilities to support the growing needs of the modern marketer as they strive to ensure that data becomes a powerful asset. Written as a practical guide, its objec-tive is to enable marketing professionals to cut through the data noise and pick the most pertinent data to tell the right story to the right audi-ence at the right time. Specifically, it will help you to:

- prioritize the data stories that matter
- develop robust, actionable and insightful data stories
- structure the data story in a way your audiences can easily navigate
- feel confident about your data analysis, interpretation and storytelling

This book has been designed as a practical guide to how to approach data storytelling and execute best practice. It will provide you with:

- the strategic planning skills to plan your data story
- the analytical skills to discover your data story
- the critical thinking skills to build the data story
- the creative skills to create data story outputs that engage and inspire
- the communication skills to deliver a data story that not only sticks but acts as a catalyst for action

In addition, the book will provide you with:

- expert perspectives from our experienced contributors
- relevant marketing examples and case studies to help you to adopt tools and adapt them to your world
- the mindset and ways of working needed to embed data storytelling into your day-to-day marketing practice

References

Belissent, J (2020) Data literacy: The secret to customer obsession, Forrester, 26 March, www.forrester.com/what-it-means/ep160-data-literacy (archived at https://perma.cc/B7FJ-5Y8L)

Campbell, C (1985) Torrent of print strains the fabric of libraries, *New York Times*, 25 February, www.nytimes.com/1985/02/25/us/torrent-of-print-strains-the-fabric-of-libraries.html (archived at https://perma.cc/2PHS-J3G9)

Klein, G (2013) *Seeing What Others Don't*, Public Affairs, New York

PART ONE

Why data storytelling is essential for modern marketing

1

The importance of data in persuasive storytelling – past, present and future

In this chapter we will explore:

- the role of data in persuasive storytelling
- how data storytelling has advanced in the 21st century
- the impact of artificial intelligence (AI) and other innovations on data storytelling

The first thing to remember, it's storytelling first and data second. Don't have your confidence dented because you see the 'data' word first. The term should be 'storytelling with data' and hopefully that should make marketers more confident because they know how to tell stories. That's what you've been trained to do. You are just using the data to make your story even better. So, I think the first thing that helps is that mindset shift about what data storytelling actually is.

Ruth Spencer, independent data leadership consultant

The role of data in persuasive storytelling

Evidence has always had a role to play in convincing others to think, feel or take a certain action. The problem is, now we have so much data it is hard to decipher what is the best evidence to use to cut through the noise and motivate others. This section looks at what we can learn from storytelling theory to help with the modern-day issue of data overload.

The classic definition of persuasive storytelling

Different data storytelling models may have unique variations but there are also some consistent components across various models – most of which align with Aristotle's principles in *The Art of Persuasion*. These principles provide a useful universal framework to refer to when defining the role of data in persuasion. Over 2,000 years ago, the ancient Greek philosopher Aristotle outlined three fundamental elements of persuasive communication: ethos, logos and pathos. These timeless principles can be effectively applied to modern data storytelling to create compelling narratives that influence and persuade audiences.

PRINCIPLE 1: ETHOS – CREDIBILITY

Ethos appeals to the audience's sense of trust by ensuring both the narrator and the evidence are credible and have authority. In data storytelling, it is crucial to establish credibility by presenting data from reputable sources and demonstrating expertise in the subject matter. Ethos also involves ensuring the accuracy and integrity of the data used, adhering to ethical standards and maintaining transparency in data collection and analysis methods.

How ethos applies to data storytelling practice:

- identifying and selecting the relevant data sources
- considering the quality, accuracy and reliability of the data
- ensuring data privacy standards
- being transparent about limitations in the data

- selecting appropriate visual formats, such as graphs, infographics or interactive visualizations, to present data in a clear and visually appealing manner
- incorporating credentials, relevant experience or testimonials from trusted experts
- validating insights gained from internal data sources with other well-respected second- or third-party data

PRINCIPLE 2: LOGOS – LOGIC

Logos appeals to the audience's rational mind and use of reasoning by providing a clearly structured and supported argument. Done well, it is easy for the audience to navigate the narrative and understand the supporting claims. In data storytelling, this involves making logical connections in data interpretation and using sound arguments to support the main message. This requires providing clear and concise explanations of data trends, patterns and correlations, and drawing logical conclusions from the data.

How logos applies to data storytelling practice:

- explaining trends, correlations and cause-and-effect relationships found in the data
- providing a perspective on the relevant context and the implications for the story
- creating a well-structured narrative that is easy to follow
- providing a point of view on what the data means and what needs to be considered
- offering a clear call to action to encourage the audience to take specific actions based on the data story – this could involve recommendations, next steps or a key ask of the audience

PRINCIPLE 3: PATHOS – EMOTIONS

Pathos taps into the emotional aspect of persuasion and is a crucial component in data storytelling – one that is often lost when simply reporting data. Given humans are not motivated by logic and evidence alone, we need pathos to drive an emotional link to the data story that will motivate the audience to think, feel and act. Pathos involves connecting with the audience on a personal and emotional level, evoking empathy and appealing to their values, desires or aspirations. In data storytelling, leveraging pathos means framing the data in a way that resonates with the audience's emotions, and using data to create mental pictures that spark their interest and engagement.

How pathos applies to our data storytelling practice:

- understanding the audience, their knowledge levels, interests, needs and preferences
- adapting the storytelling approach (not the story itself) to different audiences to enhance engagement and comprehension
- considering the emotion you want to evoke in the audience and the best way to create it
- bringing the data to life using human examples of real experiences or journeys
- grounding abstract data concepts into everyday practices that are easily understood

All three components of *The Art of Persuasion* are necessary in order to create persuasive stories:

- Drawing on pathos to motivate the audience to act will not work if there is no substantive argument to support what action needs to be taken.
- It is futile to draw on logos and provide a strong narrative if there is no credible data to back it up versus an alternative course of action.
- Providing a data dump of evidence is not going to build a strong ethos into your data story if there is no insight or meaning to help connect this with the audience.

FIGURE 1.1 The three Post-It notes challenge

How classical theory applies to the modern data story

Applying Aristotle's principles to data storytelling can bring three advantages to the modern marketer:

- It drives a clear focus on the ethical use of data and credible sources.
- It moves beyond reporting data to the restoration of evidence-based judgement and logical arguments to support data interpretation.
- It incorporates data and logical arguments alongside the importance and value of the human behaviour, needs, motivations and attitudes behind the numbers.

APPLYING THE PRINCIPLES IN PRACTICE

Figure 1.1 illustrates the three Post-It notes challenge and how it can help get initial story ideas out of your head and on to paper, while ensuring the balance between the three classic principles.

Post-It note 1 – logos question: What does the audience really to know? This question forces the data storyteller to distil and prioritize the one message that matters the most.

Some marketing examples from the logos Post-It include:

> Only by investing £5 million in paid social will we get the reach we will need in the short time frame we have available to achieve the results expected.

> Lower income doesn't equate to lower impact. Activations that bring in lower income are still worth doing as they can help to build our brand warmth prior to our big income push.

> Customers expect digital first, seamless interactions with us and have a lower tolerance for friction in our service than they do for other brands.

> The ad direction does not help Brand X mitigate the risk of attack from Brand Y because it doesn't address all of the copy issues previously raised.

Post-It note 2 – ethos question: Why should the audience believe you? This question forces the data storyteller to extract meaning from the data and justify what it is about the evidence that makes it credible in supporting the argument.

Some examples from the ethos Post-It include:

> For every X million video views we will generate X in social media revenue, meaning investment cost will be covered within three months.

> The ONS is a trusted data source and states X metric is the most reliable measure of long-term trends.

> Validated consumer behaviour in past recessions means we can confidently predict that consumers will be trading down from premium to own label, doing without indulgences and using multiple tactics to find ways to reduce spend, during the current cost of living crisis.

> Among the highest performing organizations, 80 per cent use this metric as a means to measure success in advertising effectiveness.

Post-It note 3 – pathos question: Why should the audience care?   This question forces the data storyteller to put themselves in the shoes of the primary audience and consider the emotion we want to evoke through the story. This could be any emotion – from reassurance to excitement, nervousness to shame – depending on the story message. It can tap into the commercial drivers and needs of the audience, or more human, universal motivators.

Some examples from the pathos Post-It include:

> We are driving our customers to the competition by getting this consistently wrong/failing to prioritize – our competitors don't need to do anything themselves to encourage this switch.

> By failing to intervene in a human way at this point in the journey we are escalating the issue and not giving our loyal customers the benefit of the doubt to respond positively to our messaging.

> If we get this right, we can capture this valuable section of the market and own this space before our competitors.

> Try your own three Post-It notes challenge for a story you are developing to see how Aristotle's principles can still be valuable for modern data storytelling.

How data storytelling has advanced in the 21st century

In the 21st century, where data is being generated, consumed and used all the time, the absence of data in your story will stand out. You may have a theoretically sound position, but if you can't support it with credible evidence then why should anyone be convinced by your argument? As more and more audiences become data-literate and savvy about the use of data, then the harder the storytelling needs to work to ensure data is used to support any claims and the evidence is robust and can stand up to scrutiny.

The role data storytelling plays in modern marketing

Data democratization means marketers have ever-greater access to data to help inform decisions. No longer in the hands of specialists, data is more readily available to use than ever before. Several key changes over the last decade have had a significant impact on the prominence of data within marketing as a function.

INCREASE IN ACCESS TO DATA

Access is the cornerstone of data democratization, breaking down silos and ensuring that data is readily available to all.

> What has changed over the years is the prevalence and accessibility of data and that's come with a lot of technology that marketers use in their day-to-day roles, enabling them to build their confidence in the stories they can tell, both internally and externally.
>
> **Charlotte Neal, Head of Marketing, Turning Point**

IMPROVED DATA LITERACY

To ensure that all employees can harness the power of data, organizations have invested in enhancing data literacy across the workforce. This involves providing training and resources to help marketing teams to interpret and use data effectively in their day-to-day activities.

> At the top of the funnel we can understand markets and consumers with more texture than ever before, and at the bottom of the funnel it is much easier to understand the impact of our work in detail. Who wouldn't want that?
>
> **Jake Steadman, Global Head of Market Research and Data, Canva**

DRIVE TOWARDS CUSTOMER-CENTRICITY

Organizations are increasingly recognizing the importance of aligning data initiatives with the needs and preferences of their customers. By understanding customer behaviours and preferences, marketers can tailor their efforts to deliver insights that directly impact customer satisfaction and drive business growth.

> Injecting data as inspiration before starting your marketing planning, and thinking in a customer-centric way, are key.
>
> **Sanica Menezes, Head of Customer Analytics, Aviva**

AGILITY IN MARKETING ACTIVATION

With the rise of 'always on' marketing, marketers need to be nimble when it comes to understanding what works and why. This increasingly relies on marketers' ability to quickly and effectively interpret real-time data streams to facilitate continuous improvement and optimization.

> Social media campaigns are quicker, cheaper, and often better targeted to our key audience. It was not surprising that it became an increasingly important part of the media mix. This in turn meant we had to become more agile in creating content and campaigns. It was also important to understand the effectiveness of marketing campaigns much quicker than ever before. Expectations across the business evolved and so did our data skill set.
>
> **Rosy Harrington, Global Brand Planner, De Beers Group**

INTEGRATION OF ANALYTICAL TEAMS INTO THE MARKETING FUNCTION

While many businesses will still have a centre of excellence for specific skills relating to data governance and management, it is also likely that many will have some decentralized analytical resource working directly within the marketing team. This means that senior marketers are likely to have to manage and lead analytical teams at some point in their career. In addition, the transition from a marketing role into an analytical role is becoming a recognized career pathway and an attractive option for marketers looking to get the best of both worlds and boost their opportunities as future chief marketing officers (CMOs).

> There has been a huge shift in the marketer's ability to talk an analytical and data game. You've got a lot of marketers who are becoming leaders of analytical teams because they know what they need and they can demand that quality and standard, without ever needing to have actually done it themselves.
>
> **Lizzie Harris, Customer Director, B&Q**

RELEVANCE OF DATA TO INCREASING NUMBER OF MARKETING ROLES

The evolution of digital marketing means that data is central to more marketing practices and activities than before.

> When I started working in marketing over 20 years ago, it was known that if you worked in database marketing or loyalty, you had to be data-literate. However, this field of marketing was seen by some to be second-class compared with branding or above-the-line marketing. Back then, there were many areas of marketing, such as brand management, where data literacy wasn't necessary or expected. The big shift over the last 20 years is that the number of jobs in marketing where you need an understanding of data to do the job has grown. You genuinely could do a good job in media planning 20 years ago and not know about data. Now if you're on the campaign team and buying media, you're buying impressions on Facebook and Google, and you need to understand data to be able to do that.
>
> **Ruth Spencer, independent data leadership consultant**

All the above areas of progress demonstrate that data now plays a critical role in any marketing and communication function. Data storytelling is a key enabler to make sure you are at the forefront of how that data gets used to inform decisions and actions.

The impact of AI and other innovations

Storytelling is an integral part of the human experience. People have been communicating observations and data to each other for millennia using the same principles of persuasion that are being used today. However, the means by which we can generate data and insights and tell stories has shifted significantly and will continue to do so, as technology plays an ever-greater role in our ability to collect, process and find meaning from the wealth of information available. So, what is the future of data storytelling?

> I think we've all talked about data being the engine that powers business decision-making. And there's no escaping the role that AI and data are going to play in the future. So, I think the more data-literate and aware you are, the more informed and evidence-led you can be about our decisions, regardless of what field you are in – because that is the future we're all working towards and going to embrace, right? It's about relevance and being at the forefront of cutting-edge technology.
>
> **Sanica Menezes, Head of Customer Analytics, Aviva**

The near future scenario

Imagine simply applying a generative AI tool to your marketing data dashboards to create audience-ready copy. The tool creates a clear narrative structure, synthesized from the relevant datasets, with actionable and insightful messages relevant to the target audience. The tool isn't just producing vague and generic output with questionable accuracy but is sophisticated enough to help you co-author technically robust and compelling content that integrates a level of human insight. Writing stories from vast and complex datasets will not only drive efficiency and save time, but free up the human co-author to think more creatively about how they deliver the end story to land the message, gain traction with recommendations and influence decisions and actions. There is still a clear role for the human to play as co-author, including the quality of the prompts given, expert interpretation, nuance of language and customization for key audiences. But the human co-author is no longer bogged down by the complex and time-consuming process of gathering different data sources and analysing data for insights. The human co-author can focus on synthesizing findings to make sense of patterns or trends and perfect their insight judgement and communication.

In my conversations with expert contributors, the consensus was that AI would have a significant impact on data storytelling but would never replace the need for human intervention.

The main advantages of AI for data storytelling were seen as:

- saving time for some elements of the data storytelling process, particularly data visualization and chart creation
- drilling into multiple sources of data to pull out consistent themes quickly
- identifying specific nuances from large datasets that may be missed by a human
- providing a starting framework for secondary research to build a quick picture of the overall landscape
- providing better quality do-it-yourself research, especially when creating questionnaires for surveys
- allowing more freedom and time to think about how to utilize the story to influence others

This vision for the future of storytelling is (almost) here. Tools like this already exist and are being further improved, enhanced and rolled out to market as I write this book. But the reality is that the skills involved in leveraging these tools are no different from the skills needed to currently build, create and deliver great data stories. If anything, the risks involved in not having human co-authors means that acquiring the skills covered in this book becomes even more valuable.

CASE STUDY

The experiment: Human vs machine

This experiment was conducted in partnership with the Worldwide Independent Network of Market Research and Opinion Polls (WIN), Keen as Mustard Marketing and Inspirient, an AI-driven end-to-end data analytics tool.

The brief

Using the data provided by WIN, both the AI tool and humans were tasked with preparing a presentation to the CEO and director of a global communications agency. The brief was to suggest the best stories that have come out of the research to inform a content plan that would gain maximum awareness for the research. The secondary audience for the data stories would be journalists from national media in the US and Europe, the Middle East and Africa (EMEA).

Both the AI tool and the human researchers were expected to produce a PowerPoint presentation suitable for use in a 30-minute client meeting, a press release targeting national media, a longer-form report or white paper to use as follow-up, and LinkedIn posts about the stories with suggested images.

Results

The team of humans gathered the data, organized and reviewed the key findings, pulled out the story, built a 15-slide story deck, before creating the marketing content. The total time taken on these tasks came to around *20 hours*. In comparison, the AI uploaded the raw data, analysed the data, assessed for data quality, prioritized key observations and used Chat GPT to create marketing content within *14 minutes*. Of the 14 minutes, 11 minutes was the human time involved and 3 minutes was the machine time. However, it ended up creating a 1,001 slide report and multiple presentations around the key themes.

While the human-generated press release took *2 hours* to craft, the AI-generated version took around *1 minute*, including time for the human prompts. However, the AI-generated example had a more generic story upfront, a lot of data, less focus on WIN, no quotes and was less tailored to the specific brief.

The human-generated LinkedIn article took just under *30 minutes* to create and used relevant tags, hashtags, engaging imagery and a clear focus on the story. The AI-generated example took under *1 minute* to create but was focused on the data and numbers, had no related hashtags and used data charts as images.

The data story

Despite the drive towards using AI tools in data storytelling to maximize efficiency, there is a clear trade-off between speed and relevance when utilizing AI that has an impact on quality and effectiveness. As highlighted in Figure 1.2, the reality is that human-generated insights and content are more relevant to the audience and the brief but take significantly longer to create.

FIGURE 1.2   Human vs machine? Turning WIN's data into stories

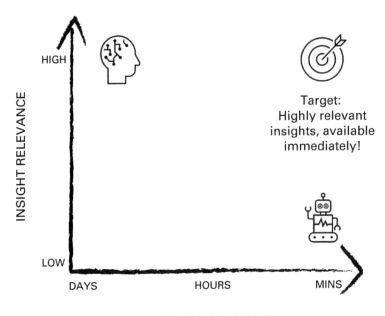

SOURCE Reproduced with permission, Guillaume Aimetti, Inspirient (2024)

In the AI storytelling exercise WIN conducted, the tool came up with '80 per cent of people are healthy' as its key point. Well, it's just not an interesting fact. Whereas the humans looking at the same data were able to see a trend of increasing stress, which is far more interesting as a story. AI could analyse the data in seconds, but my feeling is that it needs a lot of really good prompting in order for it to seriously help with the storytelling bit. I'm much more positive about it being able to create 100 slides for me from the data and that may make it easier for me to pick out what the story is.

Richard Colwell, CEO, Red C Research & Marketing Group

The ambition to achieve highly relevant content in minutes requires humans and AI working together effectively.

- Both humans and AI need to be involved in data sorting to ensure the quality of the input.

- Humans can default to AI to conduct the basic data analysis and prepare the initial content.

- Humans are required to uncover and draw out the best story from the basic data analysis, finalize the storytelling using more qualitative and human-related inputs, and create usable marketing content from the insights.

We did a recent experiment with the Inspirient AI platform taking a big, big, big dataset and in three minutes it was able to produce 1,000 slides with decent titles and design. Then you can ask it a question about anything, and it can produce 110 slides, 30 slides, whatever you want. So there is no reason why people should be wasting time on the data in that way. AI is going to make a massive difference – and then we bring in the human skill which is contextualization, storytelling, thinking about the impact and the relevance to the strategy and all that stuff the computer is never going to be able to do.

Lucy Davison, Founder and CEO, Keen as Mustard Marketing

Other innovations impacting on data storytelling

Besides AI, there are a number of other key trends that are likely to have an impact on our approach to data storytelling in the future:

- **Synthetic data** is data that has been created artificially through computer simulation to take the place of real-world data. While already used in many data models to supplement real-world data or when real-world data is not available, the incidence of synthetic data is likely to grow in the near future. According to Gartner (2023), by 2024, 60 per cent of the data used in training AI models will be synthetically generated. Speaking in *Marketing Week* (2023), Mark Ritson cites around 90 per cent accuracy for AI-derived consumer data, when triangulated with data generated from primary human sources, in academic studies to date. This means that it has a huge potential to help create data stories to inform strategies and plans.

- **Virtual and augmented reality** will enable us to generate more immersive and interactive experiences as part of our data storytelling. Audiences will be able to step into the story world, interact with the data and influence the narrative outcomes. This technology is already being used in the world of entertainment to blur the lines between traditional linear television and interactive video games, creating a new form of content consumption. Within data storytelling we can easily imagine a world with simulated customer conversations, while navigating the website or retail environment. Instead of static visualizations and charts showing data, the audience will be able to overlay data on to their physical environment and embed data from different sources accessed at a touch of a button.

- **Transmedia storytelling** will continue to evolve, with narratives spanning multiple platforms and media. Data storytellers will be expected to create interconnected storylines across different media and channels, enabling audiences to engage with the data story in different ways. We are already seeing these tools being used in data journalism, where embedded audio and video, on-the-ground eyewitness content, live-data feeds, data visualization and photography sit alongside more traditional editorial commentary and narrative storytelling. For a great example of this in practice, look at the Pulitzer Prize-winning 'Snow fall: The avalanche at Tunnel Creek' (Branch, 2012), which changed the way the *New York Times* approached data storytelling. In the marketing world, some teams are already investing in high-end knowledge share portals or embedding tools alongside their intranet and internets, to bring multiple media together in one place to tell the data story.

- **User-generated content** will also have a greater influence on data storytelling. With the rise of social media and online communities, audiences will actively participate in creating and sharing stories. Platforms will emerge that enable collaboration between storytellers and audiences, allowing for co-creation of narratives and fostering a sense of community around storytelling. Tailoring narratives to the individual audience member based on their preferences, and even their emotional state, will lead to greater expectations of customization in data storytelling to enhance engagement and impact. Moving beyond the traditional 'You said, so we did' communication with customers to demonstrate how their feedback has been actioned, user-generated content will enable customers to play a more central role in sharing their experiences and expectations.

These advanced tools are a complement to, and not a substitution for, the human creativity and critical thinking that great data storytelling requires. Used appropriately, they can enhance your data storytelling but they cannot do it for you. Whether you work with Microsoft Excel or access reports from more sophisticated business intelligence tools, such as Microsoft Power BI, Tableau, Looker Studio or Qlik, you will still need to take those outputs and use your skills as a data storyteller to curate them in ways that are useful for your end audience. There are some great knowledge-sharing platforms out there that can integrate outputs from existing data storytelling tools and help curate content in one place. Some can be built in existing platforms that might be accessible within your business, like Confluence.

Some can be custom-built using external tools for a bespoke need, such as creating a micro-site for your data story using WordPress. And some can be brought in at scale to integrate with existing Microsoft or Google tools. The list of what is available is extensive but will typically be dependent on what is available IT-wise within your own organization. What is more important is how we leverage these tools, and we will discuss this in more detail in Chapter 9.

The continuing role of the human in data storytelling

In this evolving world, the role of the data storyteller doesn't disappear but becomes ever more critical. The human data storyteller still has many important roles to play, and the skills necessary to influence and engage cynical, discerning and overwhelmed audiences become even more valuable. Now that white papers, marketing copy, internal presentations and digital content can all be generated faster than humans could ever manage on their own, the risk of information overload becomes inevitable without a skilled storyteller to curate the content.

Today, the human data storyteller is crucial for:

- ensuring we are not telling 'any old story' just because we can and that the story is relevant to the business context and needs
- understanding the inputs being used by the tool, including limitations and potential bias, as well as ensuring data is used ethically and that it is accurate, reliable and obtained with the appropriate permissions
- framing queries appropriately in the right way to incorporate the relevant context, issues and target audience needs to inform the knowledge base
- cross-referencing and synthesizing AI-generated insights or synthetic data with human expertise and subject domain knowledge to ensure relevance and accuracy of recommendations
- leveraging the different VR, AR and transmedia tools available to ensure the right one for the job

---

KEY TAKE-OUTS

1 A great data story needs to balance credible data with a logical narrative structure and an emotional connection to the insight.

2 Modern marketers need data storytelling as a key skill – being capable and willing to learn about data storytelling is a 'must have' in the majority of marketing roles.

3 Despite advances in technology, the human role in data storytelling will remain critical.

Coming up next...

In the next chapter we look at the impact of data storytelling on marketing outcomes and the benefits of data storytelling skills to marketing and communication professionals.

References

Branch, J (2012) Snow fall: The avalanche at Tunnel Creek, *New York Times*, 20 December, www.nytimes.com/projects/2012/snow-fall/index. html#/?part=tunnel-creek (archived at https://perma.cc/PV3V-4H7U)

Gartner (2023) Gartner identifies top trends shaping the future of data science and machine learning, Gartner, 1 August, www.gartner.com/en/newsroom/press-releases/2023-08-01-gartner-identifies-top-trends-shaping-future-of-data-science-and-machine-learning (archived at https://perma.cc/LRE6-S3BH)

Ritson, M (2023) Synthetic data is suddenly making very real ripples, *Marketing Week*, 24 October, www.marketingweek.com/synthetic-data-market-research (archived at https://perma.cc/8A8T-C8VF)

2

The impact of data storytelling on marketing outcomes

In this chapter we will explore:

- the role of data storytelling in creating transformative marketing outcomes
- how data storytelling can be used to persuade others to support the marketing plan
- the benefits of improving data storytelling

There are two areas where data plays a key role: inspiring marketing activity and measuring the impact of the activity to improve marketing effectiveness. This is where data storytelling is crucial.

Sanica Menezes, Head of Customer Analytics, Aviva

The role of data storytelling in creating transformative marketing outcomes

The journey from good to great

A five-year study cited in *Good to Great: Why some companies make the leap... and others don't* by Jim Collins (2001) began with a field of 1,435 companies and emerged with a list of 11 good-to-great companies: Abbott Laboratories, Circuit City, Fannie Mae, Gillette Co., Kimberly-Clark Corp., the Kroger Co., Nucor Corp., Philip Morris Cos. Inc., Pitney Bowes Inc., Walgreens and Wells Fargo. In exploring what made greatness it became clear there were a few consistent practices and a lot of myths about success that needed to be busted. One of those myths was about access to great data. Collins concluded:

> We found no evidence that the 'good-to-great' companies had more or better information than the comparison companies. None. Both sets of companies had virtually identical access to good information. The key, then, lies not in better information, but in turning information into information that cannot be ignored.

While access to great-quality data held in one frictionless data lake where anyone with any skills can access a single customer view might be the Holy Grail, the reality is that if we wait for a perfect system we will be waiting a long time. Time in which other organizations are making the most of the data they have, in whatever shape and imperfect form that comes in. This is what is necessary to gain advantage. So, if what we do with the information we have is what makes an organization great, versus merely good, then there is a central role for data storytelling to play in driving performance and growth.

The role of data storytelling in positive marketing outcomes

For a marketing team specifically, there are a number of areas where data storytelling can help transform a good marketing function into a great one. Effective data storytelling can play a key role in helping the marketing function make decisions around where to focus time, attention and effort. In this section we identify a number of positive outcomes that come from data storytelling, supported by case study examples and perspectives from our expert contributors.

BUILDING A DEEPER CUSTOMER UNDERSTANDING

By analysing demographic information, attitudes, needs, behavioural patterns, purchase history and preferences, marketers can build a stronger understanding of their ideal customer and create more personalized and targeted marketing campaigns. This in turn leads to better engagement with content and increased conversion rates. Using data storytelling to keep the organization's 'finger on the pulse' can pre-empt surprises and help spot opportunities before competitors do.

CASE STUDY

Take CeraVe as a recent example that saw potential within the beauty market that others had either missed or ignored. They were able to activate their marketing to target a specific customer segment right under the noses of some of the biggest brands who have access to a significant volume of data. While other beauty brands saw a negative impact due to Covid, according to Beauty Business Journal (2021), CeraVe's parent company reported over 40 per cent growth in its Active Cosmetics Division in 2020. The key to their success was in understanding TikTok audience data to design a marketing strategy that leveraged Generation Z skincare influencers as brand advocates. Success for CeraVe came down to using data to understand the potential target pain points and utilizing user review data to gain product feedback that could be incorporated into messaging. From this they were able to pivot their marketing investment in a timely manner to leverage the power of user-generated content on social media.

CeraVe's competitor brands have got top-end marketing teams, top of their league, and should have the best skills and tools to be all over this. CeraVe came out of nowhere because it saw market potential where the others didn't – and it knew how to activate it. CeraVe really talks to skin wellness, rather than beauty. It is all about how to deal with different skin types. So, you've got a ton of people with acne on TikTok. Then you get content creators that come along – these amazing beauty influencers that have been blogging for a long time. They've got a big presence on YouTube and they're cross-referencing that with bite-sized chunks on TikTok. The big latent pool of demand is then set on fire by these content creators. It creates a community, it lights these people up and they think 'Oh wow – that's me. That's my problem.' CeraVe used that opportunity to drive sales through to its product, because no one else in the market was doing the same.

Jeremy Hollow, Founder and CEO, Listen + Learn Research

EVALUATING AND OPTIMIZING CAMPAIGN PERFORMANCE

Marketing has evolved beyond creative intuition, and data analytics and customer insights play an ever-greater role in achieving commercial success. For example, a recent study by Boston Consulting Group, commissioned by Google (Field et al, 2019), claimed that data-driven marketing can double revenue and increase cost savings by 1.6 times. By tracking key metrics such as conversion rates, customer acquisition costs, customer lifetime value, etc., marketers can evaluate the success of their marketing initiatives. This evaluation helps in optimizing future campaigns, allocating resources efficiently and achieving better results. Data storytelling provides us with an ongoing mechanism to track and optimize business performance. By generating ongoing data stories, marketing teams can spot opportunities for tests, experiments and pilots, reviewing impact in real time, before making further interventions or changes.

CASE STUDY

A charity marketing team was charged with reducing budgets, but at the same time driving awareness, activation and income via more effective use of digital marketing. Having trialled several different campaigns and evaluating performance and impact, they had a clear indication of which events and triggers aligned best with their brand purpose and how digital marketing could support overall brand-building. However, to drive awareness among a younger audience, it was clear that aligning digital activations (such as online prize draws) with traditional media channels (such as mainstream television) was not going to work. They needed to make a case for switching budget into paid social. Using the campaign data, alongside audience insight data and sector case studies, they were able to create a data story that made the case for a specific paid social budget to support digital campaigns.

ENHANCING PERSONALIZATION

By leveraging data on customer preferences, browsing behaviour and purchase history, marketers can create customized content, offers and recommendations. This personalization enhances the customer experience, fosters brand loyalty and increases customer satisfaction.

Utilizing good data storytelling skills means we can move beyond superficial customer understanding and gain insight at a more granular level to guide this personalization. For example, measuring conversion from page views on the website to clicking through to the detailed content will give only a high-level view of what works for different customers. However, linking this learning with customer data that aligns digital behaviours with wider purchasing behaviour adds a new dimension. Then layering additional insights from user experience (UX) research that highlights how other similar targets have been triggered to act when exposed to certain messages at this stage in the journey provides an even greater level of insight to guide personalization. By getting to know customers in a much deeper way, understanding their likes, dislikes and content topics they engage with, and then feeding that back into the content plan, data can help increase the relevance and engagement of campaigns or marketing activation.

OPTIMIZING CUSTOMER EXPERIENCE

In truly customer-centric organizations the customer experience becomes everyone's responsibility. The marketing function needs to play a central role, given the importance of customer communication at every touchpoint. Data storytelling can help build awareness of the triggers, barriers and enablers along the journey and help determine what communication interventions are required for different customers at different stages of the journey.

One of the most exciting projects that we're working on in collaboration with marketing is shifting from a product-based marketing approach to a customer-centric one. From saying 'We've got to sell this product and we're going to identify customers' to being an 'always on engine' that says, 'We want to be in front of customers and the moments that matter to them.' So, it's about being relevant and responsive to those triggers and moments in our customers' lives, agnostic of the product. And it just so happens that we might have a product that is available for them. So that's a huge shift in mindset and ways of working.

Sanica Menezes, Head of Customer Analytics, Aviva

TAPPING INTO NEW SEGMENTS AND POCKETS OF DEMAND

Partnerships and affiliations are a key component of successful marketing, but knowing which influencers and demand generators to work with to tap into new target groups requires an extensive understanding of rising trends, audience sizes and brand fit, before lucrative win–win deals can be struck. Data storytelling techniques will ensure that decisions can be based on sound judgement and sustainable commercial benefits, removing the influence of the latest craze, buzz topic or senior decision-makers' personal preferences.

> These pockets of demand are out there. And if you don't get involved with it in the right way, then you're at the whim of what's happening elsewhere. I see a lot of brands trying to just invade other people's parties without really understanding what's going on. They're not really showing me that they understand the nature of the category, they're just being quirky, rather than profound. For example, before March 2020 BookTok didn't exist. Now it's one of the strongest demand generators in the young adult book category. Full stop. It's like you go into TikTok or you go into Amazon, and it's got 'As seen on BookTok'. Waterstones has a BookTok and it's ingrained in the everyday commercial experience of that brand.
>
> **Jeremy Hollow, Founder and CEO, Listen + Learn Research**

MITIGATING THE RISK OF CUSTOMER CHURN

By understanding market trends, customer preferences and competitive landscapes, marketers can make proactive adjustments to their strategies and minimize the potential impact of external factors in causing customers to churn. Whether that is identifying 'at risk' customer segments based on behaviours to trigger proactive communications, promotions or discounts, or optimizing elements of the experience based on feedback and reactions, data storytelling can have a positive impact in any retention strategy.

The retention team have managed to reduce the churn rate by 8 per cent just by implementing small data-driven changes. Things like defining when a customer is past onboarding and now at the in-life stage within the journey. Those small things made huge differences when they were starting to ask for money for campaigns, because optimizing the journey had a massive impact both on revenue and efficiency.

Rebecca Ruane, Head of Reader Revenue Insight, *The Guardian*

How data storytelling can be used to persuade others to support the marketing plan

This section looks at the positive outcomes marketing can achieve using data storytelling to influence relevant stakeholders and decision-makers both inside and outside the organization.

Drawing on case studies and our expert contributors, we will demonstrate the difference data storytelling can make in persuading others to support the marketing plan.

Utilizing data storytelling to influence internally

BUY-IN TO STRATEGY AND PLANS

Data storytelling can help gain buy-in from decision-makers and stakeholder teams to get marketing plans and strategies over the line. Buy-in and support can help protect brand assets from short-term tactics and tinkering and even build the trust needed to sell in more radical approaches.

We do a lot of work with marketing teams that are particularly interested in the Ehrenberg-Bass theory of how to grow brands. We work with one client in the National Lottery here in Ireland, who totally gets it, and uses the data to educate and persuade the board on what they want to do, because it's a very different way of thinking about marketing. For example, the value of distinctive brand assets and keeping consistency. How do you persuade a board that you shouldn't be changing stuff and that we need to keep it the same? Even simple data, such as reviewing assets and showing how confused consumers are, can help to show the strength of doing things consistently and can make a big difference.

Richard Colwell, CEO, Red C Research & Marketing Group

CASE STUDY

The 'Campaign for Real Beauty' positioning for Dove was initially rejected by senior management at Unilever because it was a disruptive strategy and did not align with their perception of beauty ideals. By investing in consumer research, the agency team at Ogilvy and the Dove brand team were able to tell the story from a consumer perspective where women from around the world expressed their views on beauty and how they felt about themselves. Ultimately, the insights gleaned from the data persuaded the board to buy in to the new positioning of widening the remit and definition of beauty. This campaign went on to be incredibly successful for the brand, supercharging their brand purpose.

In her interview with The Brand Blog (Ferguson, 2020), Daryl Fielding, who was involved in the campaign from the start, talked about the importance of spending time to get senior stakeholders on board and how this is often neglected or done badly.

JUSTIFYING MARKETING INVESTMENT

The 2023 Gartner CMO Spend and Strategy Survey indicated that marketing budgets are still below pre-pandemic levels and found that 75 per cent of CMOs are facing increased pressure to 'do more with less' to deliver profitable growth (Gartner, 2023). This means data-driven decisions around budget, resource and opportunity costs are even more important than ever.

A lot of the time, marketing feels hugely under pressure – they're being driven much more commercially than ever before. They're trying to demonstrate ROI in a world which is really fast-moving, and how do you pull apart all of the threads of what's driving this? Is it being driven by this campaign? Or is it because of that promotion? At the same time, there's data paralysis, so marketers are working with a million times more data than ever before. How do you know what to trust? How do you feel confident in what it is you're looking at?

Sinead Jefferies, SVP Customer Expertise, Zappi

As Jon Evans, Chief Customer Officer at System1 Group, states in *Marketing Week* (2023), 'something magical happens when you have significant constraints. You get creative.' In this context, a data-literate marketing team are able to use data storytelling to influence stakeholders on where money and resource are best spent to drive acquisition, retention and revenue growth.

With less budget and fewer resources, you definitely have to think differently, and you have to get stuck in more. We're always trying to find innovative ways of doing stuff. So that can be liberating, exciting, creative and motivating, but it requires more of you as an individual.

Charlotte Neal, Head of Marketing, Turning Point

Data storytelling is a powerful tool when it comes to convincing the business to give you funding and then, when you've been given the funding, assuring them that their trust will be rewarded. The best marketing directors and senior decision-makers will rightly demand that these plans are based on robust customer insight and previous performance data. The marketer needs to explain why they have taken the decision to place their budget in the different areas. Budgets are subject to scrutiny, so utilizing evidence-based insights into the effectiveness and impact of marketing efforts helps marketers justify budget allocations and secure resources for future campaigns.

GAINING SUPPORT FROM THE CHIEF FINANCIAL OFFICER

Marketing is often seen in some organizations as a cost centre with a lack of clarity on how it contributes to the bottom line. This gets even more opaque when ROI is measured in short time periods. When it comes to engaging with the chief financial officer (CFO) or other commercial stakeholders, the data storytelling effort must align marketing activities with the bigger picture.

Several recommendations were made by our expert contributors when it comes to using data storytelling to build relationships with CFOs, finance partners and commercial functions, including:

- ensure they have sight of the plan and how it fits into the bigger picture
- speak their language
- make unambiguous and relevant points
- remove subjectivity from the deliverables

Many of our expert contributors talked about subjectivity in marketing and how data storytelling can help balance the argument. One marketing expert talked about using data storytelling to mitigate the role of personal preference when making decisions regarding creative choices. Using data storytelling can align creative recommendations with consumer feedback and preference, rather than internal preference. This is critical because marketing is the function where subjectivity easily comes in because everybody has a taste, everybody has an opinion on an advert, on a piece of content, on a new logo, or on a colour used in product packaging.

The reality is that using ROI in your data storytelling is more likely to appeal to your finance colleagues than quoting marketing theory or sharing your personal preference. In fact, according to Josh Stephenson (2023), ROI is considered by two-thirds of 1,300 brand-side marketers to be the key metric demanded by the chief executive officer (CEO), CFO and other senior stakeholders to prove marketing effectiveness.

A key focus of any marketing team is to demonstrate its impact and land that message with finance and commercial teams. Proving that this proportion of sales has been driven by this marketing activity is always hard, especially in a world where there are so many other things going on. Did our revenue increase because of the range review, or this optimization we did over here, or because you put more colleagues in the store? They can all claim sales. But if you added everything up that could be claimed to influence sales, it would never equal the actual sales; it would be significantly more. So, getting financial and commercial stakeholders to believe the science, where we can share the actual result from our analysis, is really important. It requires credibility and an understanding of the science of measurement.

Lizzie Harris, Customer Director, B&Q

In the same article, Premier Foods CMO, Yilmaz Erceyes, warned that a laser focus on ROI could lead to dilution of brand equity that may 'transpire into a performance problem in the mid to long term'. So while there may be an affinity for performance data among your commercial colleagues, the data storyteller still has the responsibility to put that into context and educate the audience on the limitations of one key metric. Therefore, the more data-literate the marketing team, the more data stories can focus on the bigger picture and the different metrics beyond ROI required to evaluate performance and measure success.

Brand marketers bang on about the long and short of it. We all know brand marketing is important, but if you go in talking about the long and short of it to CEOs and CFOs, they do not care. CEOs and investors love performance marketing – one pound in and five out sounds brilliant – because you can quantify that. Apart from the large, sophisticated marketing organizations like Unilever, I still don't think marketing is fully articulated in a way that a lot of C-suite really understands, and this is really harmful. It is like an iceberg – 90 per cent of it is below the surface. The bit that's visible, because it has a pound sign and revenue against it, gets talked about more. So, you spend 90 per cent of your time talking about 10 per cent of what drives business success. There's a gap there and there are lots of examples where businesses fail because they have no real customer insight of what they want, what they are prepared to pay or knowledge of how the competition has changed.

Rhea Fox, Digital Director, Ted Baker

Leveraging data storytelling with external partners, suppliers and customers

Marketing requires strong relationships with external stakeholders to ensure the brand thrives in our hyper-connected world. Using data storytelling to influence external stakeholders is essential for those working in partnership with other parts of the value chain. Marketing needs to add value to existing datasets that the partner, supplier or customer may already have available to them through effective data storytelling.

SUPPORTING EXTERNALLY FACING COLLEAGUES TO SELL TO CUSTOMERS

Marketers can empower sales colleagues by crafting data stories that align with customer needs, market forces and brand differentiators. Utilizing data storytelling to highlight customer success stories enhances sales pitches. By sharing insights on customer preferences, pain points and market dynamics through the data story, this equips sales teams with tailored information for targeted pitches. It also helps sales to build credibility, address objections and ultimately close deals, creating a seamless synergy between marketing efforts and the sales process.

At Twitter, one of the responsibilities we had was helping our sales team sell advertising. You're selling to advertising agencies or brands, and you're convincing them why putting their work on Twitter will be the right place to spend their ad dollars. There must be data in that – whether that is big, robust, media mix modelling (MMM) type data, or whether it's data talking about the value of the audience on Twitter. If you think of any major kind of advertising moment, like Christmas, all the media owners are using a combination of data and sales craft to tell the same story. And, guess what, all that research and all those stories say that their platform is the best one for a brand to put their Christmas advertising. I would imagine it is easy for the brands to forget which media owner said what, because they're all using similar methodologies to say similar things. There's just a different logo in the corner of the slide. You have to fight to cut through that. And that's where data storytelling comes in. You can choose not to play that game, not to be just another media owner waiting in the hallway to come in and give a 30-minute presentation. You can choose to think of it differently.

Jake Steadman, Global Head of Market Research and Data, Canva (ex-Twitter)

INFLUENCING PARTNERS TO STEP OUT OF THEIR COMFORT ZONE

By surfacing emerging consumer behaviours, market trends or competitive threats, marketers can proactively adapt their marketing strategy and campaigns to stay ahead of the competition. This agility in response gives marketers a competitive edge and enables them to leverage first mover advantage, but only if they can influence partners to step outside their own comfort zone and buy in to new ways of marketing.

CASE STUDY

Traditionally the key target audience for De Beers was men buying diamonds for women, predominantly focused on the engagement ring and tokens of love. During qualitative research designed to develop a new advertising campaign, the De Beers team identified a new trend of women buying diamonds for themselves. No one in the industry at that time was speaking to this audience or pushing this narrative. Before surfacing this insight, the planning team triangulated this trend with wider macroeconomic data on female purchasing power, trend studies on the nature of modern relationships, microeconomic factors in key markets and competitor data. From this they were able to develop a compelling data story. This was then pitched to the CEO with a clear reference to the positive impact on the bottom line, as well as to jewellers around the world.

> We shared these insights in the 2017 De Beers diamond insight report which is available to the whole diamond industry. We did a feature on 'self-purchase' to create a story highlighting that this was a real gap in the market. The report had to look at consumer insight in a very different way and look beyond what we'd normally focus on. It was really important for us to think differently and highlight the synergies where we hadn't before. De Beers created a new campaign that was aimed at women, where the brand had to find a new voice for itself. We also created a new jewellery collection aimed at women and that has evolved and expanded over time and it's doing really, really well.
>
> **Rosy Harrington, Global Brand Planner, De Beers Group**

Encouraging integrated marketing plans

Producers and manufacturers need to build integrated marketing plans with the various channels to market. Personalized data storytelling can be effective in showcasing strategies to retail and other channel partners to create a win–win plan. Going beyond the sales data that the retail channel has available to them, the marketing team can integrate market, category and consumer insights and trends into the data story to recommend a tailored marketing plan. Data-driven narratives can guide collaborative promotional campaigns, optimize product placement, and refine messaging to resonate with target audiences. Sharing actionable insights through data storytelling fosters a unified approach and ensures consistency of brand message.

CASE STUDY

A governing body were looking to support the food producers they represented in their conversations with retailers and on-trade channels around the world using data storytelling to influence category-specific marketing. Looking to go beyond consumption data and barriers to purchase, the team sought to use data storytelling techniques to generate fresh insights to support above-the-line campaigns, in-store and in-aisle marketing activation. Having developed a core story that utilized extensive primary research, the organization set out to develop a number of data storytelling outputs to build the capabilities of their clients when engaging with the buyers in various channels. With an extensive data storytelling toolkit that was insightful but also easy for non-experts to use, the marketing team were able to play a key role in driving category growth.

SHOWCASING QUALITY THOUGHT LEADERSHIP

According to the B2B thought leadership impact study (Edelman, 2021), there is a tidal wave of content marketing, making it harder for companies to connect with B2B customers and prospects. Seventy-one per cent of decision-makers state that less than half of the thought leadership they consume gives them valuable insights. Utilizing data storytelling in thought leadership can help your content stand out from the noise and provide real insight.

The benefits of great storytelling are differentiation and being able to stand out when everyone's putting out content. A lot of the content is very much the same, a lot of it is just market analysis or commentary. Quite often, statistics are used without any real data storytelling. Thought leadership programmes and the content that's coming out from organizations that are doing data storytelling well are really standing out from the crowd, because they're displaying the data in a way that resonates. It's easy to digest compared to the big, long 50-page PDFs that have been the norm for thought leadership for many years. So, by breaking things up, by focusing in on particular issues, by really interrogating the data and drawing out those narratives and stories, they're showcasing their own expertise. And that's what stands out. That's what's resonating with their target markets.

Rachael Kinsella, Editorial and Content Director, iResearch Services

The benefits of improving data storytelling

The benefits of driving a data storytelling mindset

We acknowledged earlier in this chapter that data storytelling is a key tool in the journey from 'good to great', therefore the marketing function should play a central role in delivering this to the business. The marketing function is a key advocate and voice for the consumer, so taking the lead in delivering great data storytelling is a natural fit.

There are four key benefits as to why marketing should want to be focused on building the skills, capabilities, processes and ways of working to own data storytelling as a growth driver.

BENEFIT 1: DATA STORYTELLING CREATES A BUSINESS ASSET THAT HAS TANGIBLE VALUE IN ITS OWN RIGHT

Creating data stories translates data into assets that hold immense value for the organization, enabling informed decision-making, gaining competitive advantage, building customer or consumer understanding, generating revenue and optimizing performance. By developing compelling data-driven narratives, the marketing and communications team can unlock and deliver the insight to drive growth.

BENEFIT 2: DATA STORYTELLING PUTS MARKETING AT THE HEART OF BUSINESS TRANSFORMATION

Using data storytelling to encourage evidence-based decision-making, collaboration between marketing and other departments and the integration of data-driven insights into overall business strategies makes marketing the lynchpin in transforming how data is leveraged within the business. This ensures that the customer is placed at the heart of the business and every decision is referenced on the needs of the customer and aligned to operational and finance data.

BENEFIT 3: DATA STORYTELLING IS A CATALYST TO FACILITATE THINKING, CONVERSATION, DEBATE AND ACTION

By its nature, data storytelling results in a distilled and focused message, clearly communicated in an easy-to-understand output. It becomes a powerful communication tool, both inside and outside the business, by cutting out the noise, helping the audience navigate through the complexity of the data and providing meaning via human, grounded examples. Data storytelling ensures clarity and greater understanding, as the audience has to do less work to understand the message. Marketers through data storytelling can help bridge the gap between data specialist teams and non-technical stakeholders. Marrying natural storytelling skills with data analytical capabilities ensures that the organization can be more agile and confident as it takes action.

BENEFIT 4: DATA STORYTELLING IS SOMETHING WE HAVE DIRECT
CONTROL OVER

Much as we would like to make others do what we want, we are limited to influencing their thoughts, feelings and actions. We cannot make CFOs give us more money, we cannot make our sales and service colleagues support our core brand messages in their customer conversations, and we cannot make our customers like us more or buy more from us. But we can help the audience to make up their own minds by using data storytelling as a way to influence our different audiences around their own needs and wants. It is within our power to effectively analyse the data to identify the most important messages. It is within our power to decipher what data is insightful and actionable and what is just noise. It is within our power to consider how we distil and chunk our insights into easy-to-digest formats that help our audience to navigate our claims. It is within our power to evaluate and contextualize our insights within the real-world paradigm. It is within our power to choose to simplify our outputs to aid comprehension.

We will not convince our audiences all of the time, but by applying the systematic storytelling techniques covered in this book, we can be certain that this is down to other reasons and not just because they didn't understand the message in the first place.

The personal benefits of data storytelling to marketing and communication professionals

Being a good data storyteller can offer numerous personal benefits, all of which help with motivation, building new capabilities and pushing yourself out of your comfort zone. Here are some of the key personal benefits to building data storytelling capabilities gathered from the marketing delegates I worked with over the years.

ENHANCED DATA LITERACY

Data storytelling encourages you to delve deeper into data analysis and interpretation. As a result, you develop a stronger understanding of data and become more proficient in extracting valuable insights. Hands-on experience with the data can supplement and enhance any training given. By honing these skills, you enhance your critical thinking abilities and become better equipped to solve complex problems and spot new opportunities.

IMPROVED PRESENTATIONS

Presenting data in a story format makes your presentations more engaging and memorable. By combining facts, visuals and narratives, you can produce a concise and compelling story to captivate your audience, leaving a lasting impact and increasing the effectiveness of your presentations. Telling a story with the data forces us to fine-tune the main message and ensure we focus on the most important implications.

INCREASED INFLUENCE

When you can effectively present data in a story format, you can become more persuasive. Your ability to influence and inspire others grows, making you a valuable asset in various professional situations. By being a proficient data storyteller, you position yourself as a sought-after professional who can contribute to strategic discussions and drive business outcomes. This can lead to better career opportunities and advancement.

CREDIBILITY WHEN CHALLENGING OTHERS

Using evidence as part of your storytelling enables you to break through existing thinking and myths about the customer. In a customer-first business, using data storytelling to positively challenge the status quo should be actively encouraged and seen as a constructive way to achieve growth. The more capable and confident in using data, the more likely you are to identify priorities and feel empowered to push back on decisions or actions that are not supported by the evidence. Being able to make a compelling case for a particular course of action, even if not a popular one, can make a significant impact on job satisfaction, morale and sense of purpose.

EFFICIENT USE OF TIME

Having a clear roadmap to create a data story will optimize your time. Rather than spending time and energy endlessly mining data sources hoping for inspiration and getting lost on the detail, using a story framework to guide your analysis will help you to decide where to start and ultimately stop to turn around insights and ideas in a more timely manner.

KEY TAKE-OUTS

1 Data itself is not transformative when it comes to business success – it is what you do with it that counts.

2 Data storytelling will lead to a whole range of positive marketing outcomes – whether that is influencing the board, persuading external stakeholders and partners, informing customer-centric strategies and plans or reaching customer audiences.

3 Data storytelling is not going away. In fact, now is the time for marketers to invest time and energy into this skill set to reap the clear benefits.

Coming up next...

In the next chapter we look at the status quo and what needs to change, including the barriers that need to be overcome and the key skills marketing and communication professionals require to excel at data storytelling.

References

Beauty Business Journal (2021) How CeraVe became an unlikely Gen Z favorite through TikTok, *Beauty Business Journal*, 28 January, beautybusinessjournal. com/cerave-marketing (archived at https://perma.cc/86LM-R2GD)

Collins, J (2001) *Good to Great*, Random House Business Books, New York

Edelman (2021) 2021 LinkedIn-Edelman B2B thought leadership impact report, Edelman, www.edelman.com/expertise/business-marketing/2021-b2b-thought-leadership-impact-study (archived at https://perma.cc/YYQ6-Z6J4)

Evans, J (2023) What to do when you have no budget, *Marketing Week*, 6 June, www.marketingweek.com/jon-evans-no-budget (archived at https://perma.cc/ GK3G-UZRB)

Ferguson, K (2020) Daryl Fielding: The story behind Dove's 'Campaign for Real Beauty', The Brand Blog, 3 November, www.thebrandblog.co.uk/daryl-fielding-the-story-behind-doves-campaign-for-real-beauty (archived at https://perma.cc/ S6VF-RSXQ)

Field, D, Patel, S and Leon, H (2019) The dividends of digital marketing maturity, BCG, www.bcg.com/publications/2019/dividends-digital-marketing-maturity (archived at https://perma.cc/WY95-KUEV)

Gartner (2023) Gartner survey reveals 71 per cent of CMOs believe they lack sufficient budget to fully execute their strategy in 2023, Gartner, 22 May, www.gartner.com/en/newsroom/press-releases/2023-05-22-gartner-survey-reveals-71-percent-of-cmos-believe-they-lack-sufficient-budget-to-fully-execute-their-strategy-in-2023 (archived at https://perma.cc/3NHM-PG6L)

Stephenson, J (2023) ROI top effectiveness metric demanded by C-suite, *Marketing Week*, 16 June, www.marketingweek.com/roi-top-metric-effectiveness (archived at https://perma.cc/LF2T-MVQW)

3

The status quo and what needs to change

In this chapter we will explore:

- the real-world barriers to developing great data stories
- why analytical and data literacy skills matter
- the priority data storytelling skills for modern marketers

Rather than marketers thinking of data as restricting what they can do, it should be that they see it as empowering them. So maybe there's a little bit of reframing around that and the understanding of how they can use the data to better their own position, or better their position at the board, rather than seeing it as something that's telling them that they're not doing something right, or it's not working, or feeling like they are not going to be able to do X or Y, because the data is telling them not to. It's about understanding how they can evaluate the data and the strength of being able to use the data, rather than seeing it as restrictive.

Richard Colwell, CEO, Red C Research & Marketing Group

The real-world barriers to developing great data stories

Generating great data stories is not always simple. There are several blockers that get in the way of finding and telling good data stories that marketing teams need to overcome or work around if they are to leverage the benefits discussed in Chapter 2.

The role of organizational structure and culture

There are a number of issues relating to structure and culture that impact on data storytelling effectiveness.

TRADITIONAL DECISION-MAKING CULTURES

Data-driven insights often encounter resistance from individuals accustomed to traditional decision-making approaches.

> Some companies are very traditional, and they don't see the benefits that the use of data can have in driving competitiveness or creating different customer experiences. We need to do a lot to convince or to change the minds of the managers of the companies in order to increase the use of data analysis, interpretation and storytelling.
>
> **Estrella Díaz, Professor of Marketing, University of Castilla-La Mancha**

In a data-driven culture you should be knocking on an open door and being invited in to share your data stories; however, in organizations where decision-making is more traditional and often based on the experience of a handful of people at the top, trying to influence with data storytelling can feel frustrating, slow and futile.

> One of the things that I've seen is that there's so much driven by the company culture and how they operate, which comes from the top down. So, if it is a very data-driven organization that's all about dashboards and numbers then decisions must be validated by that. Or if the culture is based on instinct and goes on what feels right, decisions can be based on what people like. We've all seen the classic case of the advert that has got this person in it because it's the celebrity that the marketing director likes. So, it's driven by people's own preferences. I think a lot of marketers struggle with understanding how to get that balance right.
>
> **Sinead Jefferies, SVP Customer Expertise, Zappi**

COMPLEXITY OF MARKETING AND RIVAL CAMPS WITHIN THE FUNCTION

Across organizations, marketing departments rarely look the same and can span a wide variety of different roles and disciplines, some of which may even compete against each other when it comes to budget and strategy. Working in this type of environment adds pressure to marketers to be able to justify their point of view.

> In the old days there was just a marketing team. Then, as performance marketing really took off in some businesses, you then had a brand team over here, a product marketing team there and CRM elsewhere, which is super-unhelpful. And because measurement was the next hot thing, everyone thought brands were a bit of a waste of time and too expensive. Then they sort of came together again through tools like MMM and econometrics, but there is still a debate about 'Is it brand?' or 'Is it marketing?' I'm still seeing quite a lot of teams stuck in this debate and what has made it worse is that now we also have all the organic, social, TikTok influencer stuff, too. So, you've got all these rival camps. In one camp the talk is all about customers and is seen as a bit fluffy, and in the other the talk is all about the numbers and performance and clicks and conversions.
>
> **Rhea Fox, Digital Director, Ted Baker**

PACE OF DECISION-MAKING

In today's fast-paced world, it is hard to find time to think rather than do. This can create a pinch point where people lose focus on how to evaluate what matters and rely on simple metrics that are easier to work with. The reality is that the process of insight generation and effective data storytelling is a messy one – it may feel very circular at times and involve a few unforeseen rabbit holes. Rarely will we find a brilliant, insightful and compelling data story just looking at our screens – we need to work for it. There is no silver bullet to advance knowledge; it is about immersing ourselves and finding ways to advance. When the pace of change is fast and there is a constant expectation to be agile, move quickly or find a quick win, it is uncomfortable to feel that you are the one slowing progress down.

> It takes time and energy to shift from reporting numbers to connecting what you're seeing back into the customer and the wider organization and finding a great way to engage them with a story. Finding the space to do this can be hard, but it is incredibly worthwhile if you can do it. Marketing is a combination of maths and magic, and we tend to lose the magic because we're having to work at such a fast pace to get stuff out the door.
>
> **Charlotte Neal, Head of Marketing, Turning Point**

In addition to the pace of change in decision-making, we work in a dynamic data environment where new technologies and approaches come thick and fast. This can make it hard even for data specialists to keep up with technological advances, to stay on top of new thinking, to anticipate new developments and be able to leverage opportunities before the 'next big thing' comes along.

SPECIALISTS' TIME TAKEN AWAY FROM INSIGHT GENERATION AND STORYTELLING

The demand for data specialists, insight professionals, analysts and researchers to support marketing planning and decision-making continues to grow, but there is an increasing skills gap in the disciplines of data analytics and data science. This means there are not enough specialists available to support the marketing department as they continue to access data and harness its power. The solution for many organizations has been to invest time, resource and budget in driving data democratization, self-serve tools and data literacy training. The result is that an empowered, data-literate marketing team can create their own robust and compelling data stories without relying on resource from the traditional analytics functions. This not only speeds up the process of insight delivery, it also frees up the data experts in the team to work on cutting-edge tools, complex analysis or more strategic initiatives.

Although many data teams are growing, a significant proportion of the roles are focused on the development and maintenance of data assets, as well as servicing other business functions with their data needs. The more data is available and the more complex the data environment, the greater the amount of time and resource that goes into the upstream tasks like sourcing, cleaning and managing the data, as well as developing data products and dashboards. As a consequence, business partnering and insight translator roles become thinner on the ground and harder to justify – especially given investment in supposed self-serve tools. This means fewer experts working on the downstream tasks and a reliance on data users to manage the data storytelling tasks themselves.

> When I was leading client teams in the past, I wasn't thinking about how to structure my data assets or how to get systems in place to deliver that. But that's a real thing now – the best insight teams supporting marketing are all about systems and digital transformation, and organizing your data assets, before you can apply all of the insight skills like curiosity and storytelling and interpretation.
>
> **Sinead Jefferies, SVP Customer Expertise, Zappi**

Even insight professionals who have been recruited for their problem solving, insight interpretation and storytelling can find an ever-greater amount of their time directed to firefighting on business-as-usual projects and supporting suppliers rather than on the tasks where they can add value. I have worked with thousands of insight experts over the last decade and have found that their time to focus on proper analysis, interpretation, storytelling, communication and collaboration is even more constrained than it was a decade ago.

> The client-side Insight team are in the position to create the stories, and indeed they should be creating communication which is really engaging and exciting and helping drive conversations. But they often spend too much time noodling with the data, getting the data, checking the data, screening the data, loading into platforms, blah, blah, blah, blah, blah. They spend way too much time on the data and not developing the insight or thinking about the story.
>
> **Lucy Davison, Founder and CEO, Keen as Mustard Marketing**

WORKAROUNDS FOR ORGANIZATIONAL AND CULTURAL BARRIERS

Overcoming resistance and encouraging a shift towards data-driven decision-making requires effective communication, stakeholder engagement, and building trust in the data stories. Below are our recommended workarounds:

- Find a senior champion who already values the role of data storytelling, even if they're outside the marketing function, and build in time with them so they understand your data stories and can influence by proxy.

- Prioritize one or two key stories that need to be heard and start there. Keep reinforcing the same stories, rather than trying to add complexity into your internal communication.

- Focus on a collegiate approach to creating your data stories and draw on knowledge from across the business. This approach will be extremely valuable when it comes to educating the wider business. Be realistic – the answer to the business question is not always going to be your marketing specialism!

- Give yourself a break – having spent three years in one role trying to embed customer data and feeling like I was banging my head against a wall, I realized persistence was only getting me so far and I needed to play smarter rather than harder. This meant leveraging data storytelling skills to build a compelling message, spending less time on creating new insights and more time in conversations selling in the priority data stories.

Dealing with data issues

Poor use of data in your storytelling can have a significant impact on marketing outcomes. Making decisions without reliable data will mean more reliance on assumptions, default practices, guesswork and personal biases in your data stories. Without clear, compelling and accurate data-driven insight stories at the heart of marketing decision-making there is a risk of making poor strategic choices, investing in ineffective campaigns and a waste of resources. In addition, a lack of up-to-date data stories on customer behaviours, preferences and trends means potential for missed opportunities. Missing out on new segments, emerging trends, unmet needs and untapped opportunities can hinder innovation and growth. Using information with inaccuracies, inconsistencies or incomplete datasets can undermine the credibility of the storytelling. This feeds the fear that our insights and ideas might be misleading or that our conclusions are incorrect.

Typical problems relating to issues with the data itself that can impact on data storytelling effectiveness include the following:

NOT ENOUGH OF THE RIGHT DATA TO INFORM THE STORY
In a world overrun with data, there are still certain topics, sectors and audiences from which data is hard to obtain. Working with qualitative data only can feel especially uncomfortable when the wider organization expects numbers to inform decisions. But small data is better than no data and high-end qualitative research can trump poor-quality big data, so it still has a significant role to play in understanding customers and defining marketing strategy.

The challenges are that we get hit with a bunch of data and no context, or there's not enough data in certain areas, or certain sectors haven't been surveyed. Then you've got glaring gaps you need to manage. Also not having the right data, or not having it in a timely manner, so it goes out of date before you can do anything with it – that's no use to anybody.

Rachael Kinsella, Editorial and Content Director, iResearch Services

Parts of the marketing landscape are still less understood than others and the pace of change regarding social media platforms can make it hard for even the most innovative and forward-thinking marketer to keep up. As more energy is spent on harnessing the first-party data organizations are capturing, there is the potential to miss insights from the wider world.

There does seem to be a common thread and that's a lack of knowledge about social spaces and how quickly they can change. Talking to marketers at the moment, the biggest blind spot is the gap in their knowledge about TikTok. For me, not knowing about TikTok is the same as not knowing about Amazon, in terms of route to market and activating demand. So, the biggest skill gap is understanding the role of social spaces in the way that people make decisions.

Jeremy Hollow, Founder and CEO, Listen + Learn Research

PROBLEMS WITH ACCESSING DATA

In an organization where you have to rely on others to run a report or to develop a dashboard, this will cause delays in getting things done. This can also negatively affect your understanding of the data, how it works and what it means, because you never physically interact with the data itself. While gatekeeping is often done with good intention to manage governance and quality, it is hard to get comfortable with data storytelling if you are exposed to only a sanitized version of the data created by someone else. While some organizations have sought to build knowledge management systems and tools to work around this issue, many more organizations have very basic central repositories that can easily fall into disuse if not kept up to date or managed.

Accessibility can be really challenging, especially in a large organization, as data can start to get so siloed so quickly and there is no central repository of the customer insight that cuts across all areas, all products, etc. Being able to access data in a meaningful way can be really challenging and becomes a big hurdle. It becomes very difficult to join the dots across a lot of areas.

Sanica Menezes, Head of Customer Analytics, Aviva

DATA OVERLOAD

Data is everywhere and anyone can find a number to support their argument. The abundance of data available can overwhelm even expert data storytellers, making it challenging to identify the most relevant and meaningful insights. Sorting through large datasets and extracting key insights requires time, effort and analytical skills. But when there is so much data available it is difficult to judge where to start, where to stop, and how much of our workings out we need to demonstrate to convince others. For our end audiences, attending meeting after meeting where they are exposed to multiple metrics, spreadsheets and dashboards can turn them off data completely. This becomes even more complex when decision-makers are then exposed to different perspectives and interpretation of what the same data even means.

> When it comes to marketing and media measurement there are too many cooks. The media buying partner has their own data science and they come back with a story. The econometrics partner comes back with another narrative, and they will say to finance, 'Look, it's econometrics, it's really robust, you should believe this. They have all these different, really clever, people doing all of these different things for them. As well as our digital marketing team, we've got Google saying, 'Here's how much store sales you're driving from PPC.' The marketing director can source numbers from different teams and get a different perspective. If there is an inconsistent perspective, this can damage credibility.
>
> **Lizzie Harris, Customer Director, B&Q**

WORKAROUNDS FOR DATA ISSUES

Waiting for perfect data is unrealistic – you will be waiting for a very long time! Getting the balance between reliability and imperfection is crucial for effective data storytelling. Below are some recommended workarounds:

- Push for a hierarchy for all of the different measures that exist within your marketing world. Work as a team to understand what drives the metrics that matter most for different targets or parts of the journey and keep it simple!

- Remember that a world does exist outside your own brand bubble and look to see what relevant context can be included in your data storytelling by considering this wider world in which the consumer really lives.

- When there are gaps in the data that are absolutely critical to inform the decision, this needs to be flagged and addressed. Drawing attention to genuine gaps can prompt conversations with experts on whether the gap can be filled or whether a suitable proxy can be found.

Misunderstanding the role of data

BLIND FAITH IN DATA AND ANALYTICS TO PROVIDE THE ANSWER

In the information age we expect that data will provide an answer for everything and yet we know rationally that this is not the case.

I think over the last 10 years, there's been a massive erosion of the value placed on marketing and this is because marketers have chased headlong into data. And because they haven't charged headlong into insight. They take a data point, make a decision, which could be the wrong decision, and then they build on that. And I think the focus on data has destroyed the broader skills that marketers ought to have. It's about getting past the data and looking at the customer. Data has incredible, immense value, and the whole issue around data being like a currency has made data 'a thing'. But data is only a description or an explanation of human beings. It's an enabler to understand what's going on in terms of attitudes, behaviours, needs and markets.

Lucy Davison, Founder and CEO, Keen as Mustard Marketing

Great data storytelling requires far more than just great data. It requires us to understand the data and synthesize it against existing knowledge to join the dots. It requires us to make inferences and judgement. It requires us to know what the data can't tell us.

> There is blind faith in analytics, which is important, but it's missing these other elements. You need insight into why and where people enter a category, and then what are the stages in that process? Is the way you make sense of the world aligned to the way consumers do? I would argue that reporting on your own activity is missing a huge opportunity, that sweet spot where all the early warning signals are going to come from.
>
> **Jeremy Hollow, Founder and CEO, Listen + Learn Research**

THE FEAR OF DATA

For many non-data specialists there is a fear of data and an expectation that it is all about numbers, coding or the dark arts! This is especially true if you equate the word data with maths, spreadsheets and statistics. While there is a role for all of these things in data, these are not the areas that marketers need to worry about if they are not inclined to. It is far more important to think of data storytelling as interpretation and communication of insights driven from the data than as having to wrangle the data.

> Sometimes people can get scared because they think data storytelling means 'I've got to be able to manipulate data and do pivot tables, and as a marketeer they are not in my skill set.' Whereas in reality most marketers are never going to have to write a Power BI query. But what they do need to be able to do is know how to take all the data that they've got and construct it into a story. If you've not come from a background in data, this can look like a bit of the dark arts, and it can feel a bit scary.
>
> **Ruth Spencer, independent data leadership consultant**

WORKAROUNDS FOR PERCEPTION ISSUES

Data storytelling is not something to fear, and equally is not something that is going to answer all your questions. It is a tool, just like any other, to help you make informed decisions and to influence others. Here are two recommended workarounds to readjust your expectations of how data can help:

- Reframe data storytelling as an enabler to help you enhance your position, agenda or argument with others. See it for what it is – a useful tool in your marketing toolkit.

- Spend time with experts and ask them to demystify the data for you. Ask practical questions to find out how the data product, report or dashboard can help you solve problems or spot opportunities, rather than worrying about the nuts and bolts of the methodology itself.

The skills gap

Despite the rise in importance of data within the marketing department, the skills and capabilities to leverage this data have not increased at the same rate. In fact, according to *Marketing Week*'s 2023 Career and Salary Survey, data and analytics is still the most significant skills gap in marketing teams. In the article 'Skills gaps, wage rises, marketing tenure: 5 interesting stats from Salary Survey 2023' (Marketing Week, 2023), it states that more than a third (34.4 per cent) of the 3,000-plus respondents taking part in the survey identify it as a key area they are looking to improve. This compares to 21 per cent for content and copywriting skills, 20 per cent for social media skills and 16 per cent for e-commerce skills.

There are several issues relating to the skills gap that can impact on data storytelling effectiveness.

PRACTICAL DATA SKILLS ARE NOT BEING COVERED AS PART OF BUSINESS OR MARKETING EDUCATION

While many business schools or marketing programmes will cover the importance of understanding the customer and some will cover market research and data modules, very few offer more advanced understanding of data analytics and data storytelling for marketers. This is improving, but there is a generation of marketers who need these skills urgently. They are expected to pick these skills up and apply them to their roles, without having any formal grounding or training.

> To mitigate the data skills gap, organizations can invest in training and upskilling programmes for their employees, hire data experts or collaborate with experts in educational institutions, like universities, to build a pipeline of talent with data-related skills. I'm speaking from my own perspective working in a business school, but I think that the majority of professors in my school are not users of data, and this is still quite new for us too.
>
> **Estrella Díaz, Professor of Marketing, University of Castilla-La Mancha**

MISUNDERSTANDING OF WHAT SKILLS ARE REQUIRED

Businesses looking to fix the skills gap often focus on training in the wrong areas. Great data storytelling does not require the use of advanced tools or coding skills. The training needed combines improved data literacy skills with marketing theory and expert practice. This needs to be practical and relate to their specific organizational culture and marketing role.

> Sometimes marketers see analysts as just 'doing SQL, or Python', so they think 'If I could just learn how to do SQL, then I could do that for myself.' But you don't need to be able to do maths or code – you need to want to, and be able to, solve problems. It's learning how to get the right bit of information out to solve the problem.
>
> **Rebecca Ruane, Head of Reader Revenue Insight, *The Guardian***

Above all, it requires more training and support for marketers in the critical thinking skills that will enable them to leverage the power of data without being a data specialist.

Go beyond measurement. Are your tools and insight capabilities fully aligned to see and interpret consumer behaviour? For example, if you don't know the dominant tribes and subtribes in your category on YouTube, Instagram and TikTok then the answer is no. Do you have the skill set to do the analytics part? Do you have critical thinking and insight-generating skills to actually understand the why? Can you tell the difference between waves and tides?

Jeremy Hollow, Founder and CEO, Listen + Learn Research

WORKAROUNDS FOR THE DATA SKILLS GAP

Data storytelling is an invaluable skill in which to invest time and effort to future-proof your marketing career. To improve your data storytelling skills, here are some recommended workarounds:

- Ask for training, on-the-job coaching and to spend time with peers who already have these skills. Get familiar with the tools that you have access to and ask the owner to walk you through a practical demonstration using a live query.

- Get involved in cross-functional teams and become proactive, rather than waiting for the experts to impose their 'black box' version of the data story.

- Ask for access to relevant tools, seek out applicable sessions in industry conferences, and utilize the plethora of online courses. Think quality not quantity, and align your learnings to where will add most value to your development.

Why analytical and data literacy skills matter

The importance of analytical thinking

According to the World Economic Forum in the article 'Future of jobs 2023: These are the most in-demand skills now – and beyond' (2023), analytical thinking is in the top 10 skills in demand for 2025. The ability to analyse opinions, data and information to inform judgements about whether these are of value or not will continue to remain important in marketing teams of the future. Even in a world of automation, AI and machine learning, critical thinking skills will be highly sought after as a means to determine what information to pay attention to, what information is fake and what data is biased. The ability to navigate the data noise and determine what information is misleading is a vital skill. According to Bernard Marr in his article 'The top 10 in-demand skills for 2030' (2023), by 2030 practically all of us will be expected to understand how data affects our role, including what tools we need to use to analyse it and how to work with data fairly and ethically. Those who are able to embed these skills into their practices will be the ones doing their jobs more efficiently and effectively.

The need for data literacy skills in the marketing department

In his book *Be Data Literate* (2021), Jordan Morrow states, 'The ability to communicate data is vital to the understanding of the company's success. Overall, we can see the common theme that runs throughout the world of data literacy: everyone needs the skills to communicate with data.' Data literacy is the ability to read, analyse, interpret and communicate data effectively and data storytelling is embedded within all four of these stages. Being able to read, analyse and interpret data informs the story you need to tell and why you need to tell it; the communication of data focuses on how you tell the story to the audience. Data storytelling is something that everyone should to be comfortable with and is a practical tool to develop as part of building overall data literacy skills.

READING DATA

Data-literate marketers need to be able to read and understand the wide range of insight and data reports provided to them from other teams, external agencies and suppliers, as well as general management information. This means not just understanding the number itself, but also understanding what is behind the key performance indicator (KPI) or metric and why it is used to measure success. Also, how it is made up (if a composite score of several measures) and what influences it. From a data storytelling perspective, this will enable the marketer to use the right data for the right reasons.

ANALYSING DATA

Understanding a set of data measures and eyeballing specific numbers in a vacuum is one thing; being able to take a series of different data-sets and make sense of what they are telling you is another. With multiple datasets available to the marketing team to measure performance, position, purchase and perceptions, it is imperative that marketers understand what each dataset is saying. In addition, they also need to consider how different datasets compare to each other and explain any differences in the story. Joining the dots and synthesizing findings together will help determine what are the most important insights from the data. From a data storytelling perspective, this will enable the marketer to draw solid and robust conclusions.

INTERPRETING DATA

In a perfect world, organizations would have one single customer view, with comprehensive and complete data, and be able to make sound and accurate judgements on what the data is suggesting we do. In the real world, a single view is an unrealistic aspiration given real life and the complexity of customer touchpoints, consumer psychology and imbalanced markets. A marketer needs to optimize imperfect data to interpret meaning, generate ideas and draw conclusions. The data itself will not do this for you. It requires the human skill of making our best-informed and best-intentioned judgement based on the evidence available. From a data storytelling perspective, this will enable the marketer to have confidence and imbue trust in their data story.

COMMUNICATING DATA

Communication skills are often a natural strength for marketers. But incorporating data can unsettle even the most eloquent of content producers and presenters. But there is no point creating the most insightful, robust and actionable data story if there are no skills to communicate that story in a way that makes an impact with the relevant audience.

The priority data storytelling skills for modern marketers

The value of building data storytelling skills specifically

McKinsey (2023) cite a recent study that identified 56 foundational skills for work. Of these, 16 focus on core cognitive skills, seven of which align closely with data storytelling:

- structured problem solving
- logical reasoning
- understanding bias
- seeking relevant information
- asking the right question
- synthesizing messages
- public speaking

These are the skills that will be highly valuable to the marketing team, both now and in the future.

The data skills that marketing teams need are not the same as a data scientist, analyst or researcher. Wrangling with data and setting up data manipulation tools and platforms will not help the marketing department close the skills gap. While a data scientist, analyst or researcher might need to build capabilities in methodologies, statistics, programming languages and modelling, a marketer will gain more value from developing their knowledge of how to access the data, how to interpret it correctly, how to make judgements and decisions based on imperfect data, and how to communicate data-driven ideas and insights to others.

Priority skills for marketing and communications professionals

In conversation with our expert contributors, five core data storytelling skills surfaced as the priorities for data users in the marketing function.

KNOWING WHICH DATA TO PAY ATTENTION TO IN THE FIRST PLACE

Determining which data to prioritize and what to deprioritize is crucial. Marketers are inundated with metrics, ranging from engagement rates to conversion numbers, and not all data holds equal significance. Focusing on KPIs aligned with specific business objectives ensures that efforts are directed towards impactful strategies. Conversely, ignoring or deprioritizing irrelevant data prevents distraction and the risk of misinterpreting campaign effectiveness. The ability to sift through the noise and concentrate on actionable insights is a core competency.

> For me, the biggest gap for some marketers is being able to understand which data they should be paying attention to, and which they shouldn't. That's a big problem. And it's becoming a greater problem, because of the pressure for DIY cost-effective means of gathering data. So, they're using lots of data sources, but if they don't understand what's good data and what's bad data, then really it's just all data and it gets given equal credence in any decision-making. The biggest skill gap is being able to evaluate what they're being told from all these different sources and being able to clearly see that this bit of data is better than that bit of data. It's not that the marketers should ignore other data that's not as reliable, but it's how much weight they put on it. Ultimately, they're making huge decisions on the back of all this information, so they need to be confident that all these decisions are actually rooted in something worthwhile.
>
> **Richard Colwell, CEO, Red C Research & Marketing Group**

THE ABILITY TO CHALLENGE AND QUESTION THE DATA

Blindly accepting data without questioning its validity or relevance can lead to misguided conclusions and suboptimal choices. The capacity to challenge and question data ensures that marketers identify potential biases, anomalies, or inaccuracies that may distort their understanding of market dynamics.

> I think the good marketers are the ones that can challenge if the number doesn't look right, or it doesn't make sense, or it's not big enough to be significant. They understand the methodology to the point that they can

explain it to other people credibly and answer questions on it when challenged. They can read patterns and analyse the data, challenge the data if they need to – asking questions around significance and knowing what it means, or asking how robust the control group was.

Lizzie Harris, Customer Director, B&Q

DRAWING INSIGHT, MEANING AND ACTIONS FROM MULTIPLE DATASETS

In the complex landscape of modern marketing, data is often sourced from multiple channels, such as social media, sales channels, customer surveys, website analytics and other touchpoints. The ability to synthesize this disparate information enables marketers to identify nuanced patterns, correlations and hidden opportunities that may go unnoticed when examining individual datasets. By combining insights, marketers create a holistic view of their audience, allowing for more precise targeting and personalized campaigns. Synthesizing data helps marketers uncover the interplay between various factors influencing consumer decisions.

Every single marketer will be making decisions on a continuous, if not minute-by-minute, basis, based on data, because they're doing digital marketing. They'll be looking at Google Analytics or they'll be looking at their website performance, the UX as well as non-digital data in terms of sales and performance. But a marketer should be looking at multiple different data sources at any point in time and be thinking about how to tell their story to the business to get their idea over the line, and if it's not grounded in insight then I don't think it's going to go anywhere.

Lucy Davison, Founder and CEO, Keen as Mustard Marketing

BEING ABLE TO DIG DEEPER

Discerning subtle differences within the data can help marketers refine their messaging, tailor content to specific demographics and anticipate changing preferences. This level of detail enhances the effectiveness of marketing strategies, making them more attuned to the dynamic nature of consumer expectations. Recognizing the nuances within data also aids in uncovering untapped market segments or niche opportunities. In a landscape where personalization and relevance are paramount, the ability to be able to look beyond the obvious and dig below the surface can make the difference to the quality of the final outcome.

> Scrutinizing survey findings, making something interesting out of them, combining it with qualitative interviews and subject matter interviews, pulling all those different threads together to build the bigger picture and to create the stories, is still quite a niche skill set.
>
> **Rachael Kinsella, Editorial and Content Director, iResearch Services**

UNDERSTANDING ENOUGH TO EXPLAIN IT TO OTHERS

Complex concepts, abstract methods and technical terms all inhibit great data storytelling. Finding ways to communicate to non-technical audiences can be challenging. Complexity can be overwhelming, and a great storyteller needs to find a way to translate the insights in an accessible way, without over-simplifying the insights themselves.

> I also think it's about really having a grasp and a mastery of your data. There's something important about feeling comfortable with data. And even if data and analytics are not your strong point, find somebody who can help you understand what that means. You need to be able to look at a dashboard and go, 'I know what this means. I know what this is telling me. I understand how to look at these metrics.' If it's your strong point, great, but if it's not, find somebody who can help you feel comfortable with what that is. So, you can trust your instinct on what it is that you're seeing in the data.
>
> **Sinead Jefferies, SVP Customer Expertise, Zappi**

KEY TAKE-OUTS

1 You need to find ways to work around the various blockers to great data storytelling, rather than wait for the perfect environment.

2 Investing time and energy in developing analytical and critical thinking skills will future-proof your skill set – but this doesn't mean you need to become an expert statistician or coder.

3 The core skills for great storytelling focus on understanding data, finding meaning from the data and being able to clearly communicate.

Coming up next...

In Part One we have looked at why data storytelling is important, including the benefits it provides and the barriers we need to work around to instil a data storytelling mindset. In Part Two we will look at how to develop a great data story in practice using the data storytelling roadmap. Each chapter takes you through a step in the roadmap and provides practical hints and tips for creating a persuasive data story.

References

Marketing Week (2023) Skills gaps, wage rises, marketing tenure: 5 interesting stats from Salary Survey 2023, *Marketing Week*, 17 January, www.marketing-week.com/skills-wages-tenure-5-interesting-stats-salary-survey-2023 (archived at https://perma.cc/JSJ4-89FW)

Marr, B (2023) The top 10 in-demand skills for 2030, *Forbes*, 14 February, www.forbes.com/sites/bernardmarr/2023/02/14/the-top-10-in-demand-skills-for-2030 (archived at https://perma.cc/9YZ4-SWUJ)

McKinsey (2023) What is the future of work?, McKinsey, 23 January, www.mckinsey.com/featured-insights/mckinsey-explainers/what-is-the-future-of-work (archived at https://perma.cc/W3PU-MDLC)

Morrow, J (2021) *Be Data Literate: The data literacy skills everyone needs to succeed*, Kogan Page, London

World Economic Forum (2023) Future of jobs 2023: These are the most in-demand skills now – and beyond, World Economic Forum, 1 May, www.weforum.org/agenda/2023/05/future-of-jobs-2023-skills (archived at https://perma.cc/Q8XV-MEHJ)

PART TWO

How to develop great data stories

4

Defining great data storytelling

In this chapter we will explore:

- the 5Rs roadmap to a great data story
- the benefits of the 5Rs roadmap
- how to use the 5Rs roadmap

In my experience of working with businesses around the world, I have found that companies that are better at simplifying the outcomes and the story are more successful than the ones who aren't.

Richard Colwell, CEO, Red C Research & Marketing Group

The 5Rs roadmap to a great data story

Part One of this book outlined the need for data storytelling, the benefits of data storytelling for the marketing function, and the practical barriers that can get in the way of creating a great data story. Part Two answers the question: 'What do I need to do to create a great data story in practice?'

The 5Rs roadmap is summarized in Figure 4.1. It has five key stages with expected outcomes, each supported by three practical steps. For a more comprehensive colour version of the roadmap visualization, please visit www.datastorytellinginmarketing.com.

FIGURE 4.1 The 5Rs roadmap

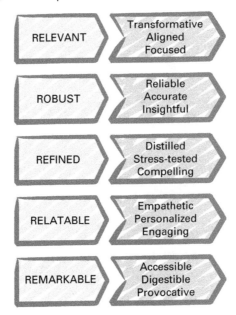

The outcome is a great data story that is:

- relevant
- robust
- refined
- relatable
- remarkable

Chapters 5 to 9 will take you through each of the 5Rs in detail, but below there is a summary of each stage.

Make it RELEVANT

A relevant data story must focus on the audience's knowledge levels, needs and preferences and should include:

- a clear premise that will generate a *transformation* in the hearts and minds of the audience

- a clear understanding of the context *aligned* to the audience's needs
- a *focused* story that answers the killer question for the audience

A relevant story requires *strategic thinking skills* to outline the story *plan*.

There are several benefits to this stage, including:

- the opportunity to gain early input, collaboration and co-creation to feed into your story development
- a clear sense of purpose to keep your story development on track
- a chance to get nearer to right first time, thus saving significant iteration time at the later stages of your story development

Chapter 5 provides more detail on how to make your data story relevant.

Make it ROBUST

A robust data story must stand up to scrutiny and should include:

- a solid interpretation drawn from a range of *reliable* data sources
- a data-driven argument and recommendation based on *accurate* and up-to-date information
- an *insightful* point of view providing the audience with a 'So what?' and 'Now what?'

A robust story requires strong *analysis skills* to surface and *discover* the key insights.

There are several benefits to this stage, including:

- the opportunity to uncover new insights and ideas, rather than predictable findings
- a chance to draw out richer, nuanced insights that can give depth to your data story
- a sense of confidence in the credibility of your interpretation and recommendations

Chapter 6 provides more detail on how to make your data story robust.

Make it REFINED

A refined data story must provide a clear and compelling narrative and should include:

- a story resolution that is synthesized and *distilled* into a key message
- a *stress-tested* story resolution that can drive real decisions and actions
- a *compelling* structure that makes it easy to follow the argument

A refined story requires *critical thinking skills* to *build* a data story that is easy to follow and engage with.

There are several benefits to this stage, including:

- the chance to pinpoint the specific ask the data story needs to get across to the audience
- a sense of confidence that your data story offers the audience solutions that are both commercially viable and practically feasible
- the opportunity to focus your audience on decisions needed or actions required, rather than all of their energy being used to understand the insights

Chapter 7 provides more detail on how to make your data story refined.

Make it RELATABLE

A relatable data story needs to enrich the insight message with an emotional connection and should include:

- an *empathetic* understanding of the humans involved in the data story
- a *personalized* approach that speaks to the specific target audiences' hearts and minds
- an *engaging* story flow that draws the audience in

A relatable story requires *emotional intelligence* to *create* a story grounded in real life and enriched by human experience.

There are several benefits to this stage, including:

- the increased likelihood of cutting through and resonating with the audience
- the chance to influence real results and meaningful outcomes
- a sense of confidence in your ability to integrate data, logic and emotion in your data storytelling

Chapter 8 provides more detail on how to make your data story relatable.

Make it REMARKABLE

A remarkable data story must cut through the noise, land the message and provide a catalyst for action and should include:

- an easy-to-follow and *accessible* data story presentation
- a range of *digestible* micro-content that appeals to a wide range of audience needs
- a storytelling delivery that is *provocative* and stimulates reflection and debate

A remarkable story requires *creative thinking and flair* to *execute* a story that will stand out from the crowd and drive action.

There are several benefits to this stage, including:

- the ability to keep a distracted audience's attention
- the opportunity to drive further interest in your data story
- the chance to disrupt the status quo and move beyond default thinking

Chapter 9 provides more detail on how to make your data story remarkable.

The benefits of the 5Rs roadmap

There are several advantages to the roadmap.

Practical

This roadmap has been tried, tested and fine-tuned over many years with different functions and teams. By breaking it down into 15 different steps across the five stages, it can be easily incorporated into existing processes and ways of working in teams depending on need. For example, on a strategically significant data story, such as onboarding retail partners with brand plans, each step will require more dedicated time to ensure a best-in-class persuasive story than if you are sharing insights with a marketing peer.

Flexible

The steps are flexible, enabling you to adapt your data storytelling approach to different scenarios. For example, if you work closely with insight business partners or analysts within your team, you may need to be less hands-on at some of the stages. If you have expert visualization support, you may not need to invest time in learning the tools to execute a great data story but will need to know enough to brief those who can help you. You might not be called on to deliver the story but may need to prepare a story that your manager or the senior director in the team will deliver. For different stories and on different occasions, some skills and tasks will require more of your time and effort than others.

Holistic

The telling of the story is just one step in the data story roadmap. By also focusing on how to effectively plan your story, surface real insight, build a narrative and create a well-rounded data story, you can be confident that you are communicating stories that are worth telling. There is no point in having a beautifully executed story that is meaningless, flimsy and irrelevant to the audience. By covering all stages in the journey, the roadmap enables you to leverage your existing strengths and dial up efforts in areas that need further improvement.

How to use the 5Rs roadmap

Each of the following chapters in this section will outline the stages and steps in the roadmap in more detail, including why they matter and how to implement them in practice.

As your guide through this 'how to' section, I am assuming that you know your own audiences, stakeholders, domain specialism, commercial goals and marketing practices, and that you will use the hints and tips as required, adapting to the individual needs of your role, team ways of working and specific projects. To support you with adapting your data storytelling approach, you can find a range of different examples across different contexts for each step, so you are able to draw inspiration from real-life practice, as well as more detailed case studies that provide a comprehensive perspective on how others have used the roadmap to help with their data storytelling.

Each chapter also has some practical elements, with a reflection exercise to enable you to review, audit and improve existing data stories, as well as an implementation challenge to put the steps into practice when creating a new data story. I encourage you to spend time trying these practical tasks to see how the steps work for your own data stories and to be able to use this real-world application to help you refine, perfect and scale your data storytelling.

5

How to plan a relevant data story

In this chapter we will explore:

- the power of a relevant data story
- the pitfalls to avoid when planning your data story
- the three steps to best practice
  - ○ identify the story transformation
  - ○ align the story premise to the bigger picture
  - ○ focus on a killer question
- putting into practice

The power of a relevant data story

QUICK RECAP

A relevant story requires using our strategic thinking skills to outline
an initial story plan. This story plan enables opportunities for early
collaboration, provides us with a clear sense of purpose and helps avoid
needless iteration.

Making a difference

The case study example below demonstrates the value of developing a relevant story plan before diving into the data.

CASE STUDY

Context

A marketing client in the grocery retail sector needed to develop a data story to convince their executive committee to shift their marketing stance in light of the cost-of-living crisis. Despite the wealth of data the marketing team had available to them, they were unable to cut through and disrupt default thinking about the brand and the customer. They needed a new data story to challenge these myths and inject a sense of urgency into the current marketing plan.

Challenge

By auditing their existing data stories, it became clear there was an issue with relevancy:

- There was a disconnect between the different brand measures tracked and the ultimate KPIs the executive committee cared about.
- There was no clear connection between the different brand measures themselves, resulting in mixed messages, where some measures were holding ground, some losing ground and some appearing to improve.

This lack of clarity surrounding relevance to the bigger picture made it difficult to get across the need to take decisive action.

Action

To develop a plan for the data story we set up a 90-minute workshop with a select group of the marketing team and their insight partners.

Data storytelling priority number one

The team realized the most important task was to clearly define the parameters for the data story and how this would align with what mattered most to the audience. Given grocery retail is highly competitive and the brand's current position in the market, the number one priority for what was already shaping up to be a difficult trading year was to protect market share from the nearest competition. This became the 'north star' we needed to align to.

Data storytelling priority number two

Next, the team needed to be ruthless in the distillation of what we were measuring and what was in and out of scope for the story, given this 'north star'. Rather than looking to tell an exhaustive story explaining all the data, we agreed to develop a hierarchy of measures. The brainstorm resulted in the identification of one lead brand indicator to measure performance, three key levers as drivers of the lead indicator and two clear customer segments where these measures mattered most. The purpose of the data story was to drive a transformation in the understanding of the executive committee around these priorities. Everything else was noise.

Data storytelling priority number three

To drive this transformation in understanding, the marketing team were going to have to bust some pre-existing myths. The key challenge was to overcome the disconnect between how the brand was really perceived versus their main competitors in the current trading environment and how the executive committee felt shoppers viewed the brand. Highlighting this disconnect was a big focus of the data story, as we needed to get across the vulnerability of the brand if we were to get them to understand the need for different marketing interventions.

Data storytelling priority number four

The marketing team needed to be unambiguous on which specific promotional tactics they would be recommending in the data story. This would mean providing clear direction on the actions that would make the biggest difference to the key drivers among the priority segments.

Results

The workshop felt uncomfortable at times. The multitude of measures had become a comfort blanket. But this level of planning was going to be instrumental in the ultimate success of the data story. Once this plan had been agreed at the end of the workshop, the process of analysis and story building became significantly easier for the marketing team and their partner agency to do. In the final data story, we identified six promotional tactics that still aligned with the brand position for the longer term but would ultimately lead to protecting share during this difficult period. While some of the tactics aligned with existing plans and provided some reassurance that actions already in place would make a difference, the data story also introduced new tactics focused on removing friction around certain offers, changing target messaging as well as making some tweaks to the loyalty programme to ensure that discounts were competitive.

Outcomes and learning

By focusing the data story on a more succinct and targeted message, the marketing team were able to make some clear asks of the executive committee. In addition, the story planning session informed the marketing team's plan to measure the success of the interventions that were signed off so they could evaluate what worked in practice. A frustrating and uncomfortable 90 minutes of planning led to a successful outcome and saved a significant amount of pain in developing this and future data stories.

The pitfalls to avoid when planning your data story

There are three main pitfalls to avoid when planning your data story:

- providing generic context
- failing to scrutinize the query for the real question
- looking to retrofit data stories to support existing ideas and actions

Providing a generic context

A generic context lacking in relevant details will not resonate with the audience, leading to decreased engagement with the data story from the outset. By failing to connect with the wider context, the data story will not result in the emotional response required to motivate action. A data story that relies on generic context, without consideration of the nuances for the particular brand, product, service, customer or business challenge, will lack depth. This can leave the audience questioning the relevance to their unique situation. To create impactful data stories, marketers and communication professionals should focus on crafting narratives that are relevant, authentic and tailored to the specific needs and interests of their audience.

Failing to scrutinize the query for the real question

Poor business questions lead to poor data stories. Overly broad and ambitious stories can lead to a data dump of everything you can uncover about a subject, while a request that is too specific leaves no room to consider the wider context, drivers and alternative needs. Often, a poor question will trickle down from the top and no one knows why the question is important or the reason is lost in translation. This is called the HIPPO effect (highest paid person's opinion), and a HIPPO question can often be taken as important only because of who has asked it, rather than because it is a worthwhile question to explore.

For example, while training a senior management team on the importance of asking good questions, a senior commercial director complained that when he asked questions of his marketing analytics team, he was often provided with a huge volume of findings, rather than an actionable insight. When pushed to share an example question, he stated he had asked the team to share insight on a specific target group. When challenged, it was clear he had not shared any context as to why this group was important or what decision this knowledge would feed into. In the absence of better guidance, the team did exactly as requested. This resulted in a large PowerPoint deck of slides containing a significant number of data visualizations. However, if the senior manager had shared more reasoning and had asked a better question, he would have received more valuable customer insight and a data story that could influence action. In this case, his real need was to understand the behaviours of this target group just before they let their membership lapse, in order to identify marketing interventions that could be triggered before attrition.

Poorly crafted questions can lead decision-makers in the wrong direction, as they fail to capture the essential information needed to make informed choices. In problem-solving scenarios, poor questions can hinder progress by:

- failing to uncover the root causes or underlying issues
- addressing symptoms rather than the actual problems
- wasting valuable time, effort and resources

Looking to retrofit data to support existing ideas and actions

Rubber-stamping ideas and actions that are in play misses the opportunity to tell a data story that is truly consumer- or customer-centric. Biased or leading requests can influence teams to deliver answers that align with the questioner's agenda or desired outcome, compromising the objectivity of the data story. Valuable insights may be overlooked if you do not explore the wider context, different perspectives or findings from the datasets.

The three steps to best practice

1 Identify the story transformation.

2 Align the story premise to the bigger picture.

3 Focus on a killer question.

In this section we will look at each step in turn, including why it matters and how to implement in practice.

Step 1: Identify the story transformation

WHY DEFINE THE TRANSFORMATION?

A premise is the key to any story. Your premise is the underlying idea of your story; the foundation that supports your entire plot, your point of view from your analysis and how you position this in any creative output. According to J D Schramm (2020), 'Every good story charts a change – even a subtle one'.

If stories are about transformation, then a good plot will guide the audience through that transformation. But, as the creator of the story, you need to be clear about what that transformation will be. Your first step is to define the impact you seek through your story. At the most fundamental level, the change that your data story should support is the recognition of the truth. What is not known, understood or believed before the start of the story should be known, understood or believed by the end.

HOW TO DETERMINE THE TRANSFORMATION

Data storytelling has the power to create various audience transformations, impacting how individuals perceive, understand and act upon information presented through data-driven narratives.

Start by asking yourself the question:

> What transformation in the hearts and minds of the audience does my story need to inspire?

To answer this question, you need to complete two tasks:

- Do your homework on the audience.
- Reflect on typical transformation examples.

DO YOUR HOMEWORK ON THE AUDIENCE

Here are five questions to ask yourself about the audience for your transformational story:

- Who is the primary audience?
  - Identify the specific individuals or groups who will be hearing or reading your story.
  - Consider factors such as their demographics, roles, interests and prior knowledge related to the subject matter.
- What is their view on the topic now and where do we want it to be?
  - Understand the audience's needs, challenges and aspirations.
  - Determine what topics or themes are most relevant and engaging for them.
- What emotions do you want to evoke?
  - Consider the emotions you want your audience to experience and what will be necessary to open minds and provoke thinking and debate.
  - Transformational stories often aim to evoke emotions such as inspiration, empathy, hope or determination. But they might sometimes leverage fear, shame or nervousness to disrupt patterns of thought.

- ○ Think about how these emotions align with your audience's mindset and motivations, and what has worked or failed in the past.
- What do you want them to take away from the story?
  - ○ Define the key message you want your audience to remember about the topic. Whether it's a call to action or a change in perspective, ensure that the message aligns with the transformational impact you seek to create.
- How can you make the story relevant?
  - ○ Find common ground with your audience to make the transformational story relevant to their own experiences.
  - ○ Incorporate elements that resonate with their lives, challenges or aspirations, so they can see themselves reflected in the narrative.

By asking these questions, you can gain valuable insights into your audience's mindset and tailor your transformational story to connect with them on a deeper level. Your homework will be invaluable at later stages in the data storytelling roadmap as you position your message and create story mechanics that relate to the audience.

REFLECT ON TYPICAL TRANSFORMATION EXAMPLES

Here are some example transformations that can be achieved with data storytelling:

Transformation 1: From confusion to clarity

- Data can be complex and overwhelming, especially for non-technical audiences. Data storytelling can transform confusion into clarity by presenting data in a more accessible and understandable format. Through compelling narratives, data storytellers can break down intricate concepts and findings into digestible insights, helping the audience grasp the key takeaways. In this situation your realistic and achievable premise for your story might well be to drive awareness of the challenge and how the data can help understand the issues and potential options, and very little else.

Transformation 2: From disconnected facts to holistic understanding

- Data points in isolation will not provide a comprehensive picture. Data storytelling can transform disconnected facts into a holistic understanding by contextualizing data within a broader narrative. By showing the relationships and patterns between data points, data storytellers enable the audience to see the bigger picture and make more informed connections. In this instance you need them to shift from being aware of some of the disconnected facts to a holistic understanding of what needs to be done to address a problem or leverage an opportunity.

Transformation 3: From apathy to engagement

- Numbers and statistics alone may fail to capture the audience's attention or evoke an emotional response. Data storytelling has the ability to turn apathy into engagement by weaving a narrative around the data. By connecting data to real-life examples, anecdotes or human stories, data storytellers can make information relatable and emotionally resonant, keeping the audience invested in the story.

Transformation 4: From scepticism to conviction

- Scepticism about data and its interpretation is common, especially in decision-making processes. Data storytelling can transform scepticism into conviction by presenting data-backed evidence and logical arguments in a compelling manner. When data is used effectively to support a narrative, it can build trust and credibility with the audience, leading them to embrace the insights. You may well have an audience that fully understands the course of action you are recommending from the data but are sceptical that this is the best route forward. The actions may be contrary to what they already expected or have invested time, resource and budget in. They might be sceptical of the data itself, especially if it doesn't relate to their own world view. Sometimes it can take a significant amount of time to progress a story from scepticism to conviction – but without this belief the audience are not going to be prepared or motivated to act.

Transformation 5: From resistance to willingness to change

- Change can be met with resistance, especially if it challenges the status quo. Data storytelling can transform resistance to change by using data to illustrate the need for adaptation and improvement. When data is used to demonstrate the benefits of change and address concerns, it can facilitate a more positive and receptive attitude towards necessary action. Sometimes the resistance is due to an unwillingness to change among the audience, while sometimes it is due to real barriers. Acknowledging that change is difficult in your data storytelling, and providing examples of how others have worked around these challenges, shows empathy for the audience.

Transformation 6: From complacency to action

- Mere presentation of great insight is not enough to drive action. Data storytelling can inspire action by creating a sense of urgency or highlighting the potential consequences of inaction. By outlining clear opportunities or challenges revealed by the data, data storytellers motivate the audience to take specific actions. It's only when your audience are engaged with the insights, and have conviction in the recommendations and a willingness to change, that your story can nudge them to take action. At this stage our story doesn't need to convince; it needs to compel the audience to turn the data story into a reality.

It is important to be realistic about what transformation your story can inspire. While you may want to drive action from your story, if the primary audience is still confused about the facts relating to the topic, it is unlikely that your data story will get them to walk away ready to take immediate action. Expecting them to go from unaware to action through one piece of communication is unrealistic – human beings just don't work that way.

> To answer the question:
>
> What transformation in the hearts and minds of the audience does my story need to inspire?

Try completing the following sentence:

After delivering my story on [TOPIC], my primary audience [WHO], will have shifted from [CURRENT POSITION] to [EXPECTED POSITION], resulting in [CHANGE].

For example:

After delivering my story on the value of paid search, my primary audience, the director of marketing, will have shifted from resistant to being willing to use this campaign to trial paid search and will support budget sign-off.

After delivering my story on customer perception of brand partnerships, my primary audience, the head of partnerships, will have shifted from being sceptical about the role of customer perception versus commercial results in determining who to partner with to being convinced that some partners generate more brand equity than others, resulting in a review of the decision-making criteria.

After delivering my story on brand performance and the impact of our value strategy, my primary audience, the board, will have shifted from complacency to action, resulting in the removal of barriers to access promotions.

Step 2: Align the story premise to the bigger picture

WHY ALIGN TO WHAT MATTERS MOST?

At the heart of transformative storytelling is the illumination of ideas with context – whether that is the macroeconomic context, the market context or the strategic context. Great data stories work because they don't just tell the story from the datasets in a vacuum; they orientate and align to the issues that the specific audience cares about. By aligning to what matters most you can deepen understanding, reframe knowledge and reveal new perspectives on common issues, challenges or opportunities that already mean something to your audience. Through understanding strategic priorities, lead indicators, predictors of performance and existing impact measurement frameworks, you can highlight the relationship between these wider goals and your day-to-day practices to find your data story sweet spot.

The best kind of marketing leaders have got that real sense of what a company is trying to do, but also understand what the role of marketing is in driving that. It's all about getting that understanding of what the core business focus is, what are the questions that you're trying to answer to support that, and being really, really clear about your role.

Sinead Jefferies, SVP Customer Expertise, Zappi

Finding the connection between the data story and the metrics that matter most enables your story to remain relevant. By conveying the key insights and implications of the data story in a way that is relevant to the audience it will:

- reach the audience on a personal level
- foster better understanding
- demonstrate a clear link between the analysis and desired outcomes
- encourage them to take more accountability
- identify the most promising business opportunities

Aligning our data story to the marketing strategy, the broader customer strategy and overall business strategy enables us to maximize its reach, impact and value. This ensures that time, effort and funds are directed towards marketing and communication initiatives that are likely to have the greatest impact on business outcomes.

HOW DO I ALIGN THE DATA STORY PREMISE TO THE MOMENTS THAT MATTER? Start by asking yourself the question:

How will this data story create value for the business?

To answer this question, you need to complete two tasks:

- identify the relevant source of value
- define the problem statement

IDENTIFY THE RELEVANT SOURCE OF VALUE

There are only five sources of value for a business. Knowing which one our data story relates to is a quick shortcut to aligning to what matters the most.

Acquisition

- Your marketing efforts to enter new markets, drive switching from competitor brands, gain new customers to try your products and services, and reach new targets and lapsed customers all feed into the topline driver of revenue through acquisition. Any data story that is evaluating your ability to reach and convert new customers needs to clearly spell out the alignment to your overall acquisition goals and targets.

Retention

- Your marketing efforts and customer communications strategy supporting satisfaction, repeat purchase and loyalty all feed into the topline driver of retention. Any data story that is helping your ability to reduce churn, drive renewals or repeat usage, encouraging loyal behaviours, such as advocacy and recommendation, needs to clearly spell out the alignment to overall retention ambitions and targets.

Upsell/cross-sell

- Your marketing efforts to encourage existing customers to buy more, upgrade, or purchase adjacent products and services in the range or portfolio all feed into the topline growth driver of revenue through increased customer spending. Any data story that is focused on optimizing communications with customers to build and convert incremental revenue needs to clearly spell out the alignment to like-for-like growth targets.

Cost saving

- Your marketing efforts to drive customer behaviours into more commercially effective communication channels and routes to purchase all feed into the bottom-line profit driver of cost savings. Any data story that is focused on evaluating how well you are transitioning traditional communication into digital channels or optimizing marketing spend needs to clearly spell out the alignment to budget reduction or efficiency targets.

Risk reduction

- Your marketing efforts to utilize the most relevant communications channels and efficient media mix and create the most compelling marketing messages for the budget available all feed into the bottom-line profit driver of risk reduction. In addition, data stories that evaluate success of brand building and the ability to ward off current and future threats also align to risk reduction. In a world where money is spent and invested just to keep the doors open and operations running, aligning your stories to how you can optimize the investment both immediately within a fiscal year and over the longer term to ensure sustainable growth is going to be attractive. Any data story that is focused on providing a good return on investment, how to improve returns or how to build brand resilience needs to clearly spell out the alignment to short-term and long-term ambitions.

Marketers need to understand the commercial objectives. Marketing can be powerful because you can deliver any objective you need or want, so knowing the strategy enables you to come up with the best plan to deliver results. For example, if you go to a buyer and ask for £20,000 of their margin and say 'We will turn it into £50,000 of incremental sales', that might not be a good deal for the buyer based on their objectives. Maybe they are already on target for sales and profit and don't need to give up margin. Maybe their strategy is to gain new customers to the category rather than incremental sales, or they need to improve the relationship with a particular supplier to get more funding. Every category has its own agenda, and it is important to spend the time understanding this, rather than assuming.

Lizzie Harris, Customer Director, B&Q

DEFINE THE PROBLEM STATEMENT

Diagnosing the problem you are helping to solve with your data story requires you to focus on both internal and external sources of pressure. In addition to understanding what these pressures are, you also need to evaluate and spell out the impact, especially on your overall goals and aspirations. Some of the challenges will be known to the audience and some only become apparent once you have completed your analysis of the data. Some problems at a macro level may be hugely influential but might be outside of your control to change and require the business to review how to respond; some are within your control and require you to consider specific decisions and actions.

Try asking yourself and your stakeholders the following questions to define the problem statement:

- Why is this an important story to tell right now compared to the other stories you could tell?

- How does this data story help you better understand your customers and their needs/expectations/behaviours and how you respond to these?

- What macro-level factors are relevant to this story and how will the data story help the business leverage/overcome these wider factors?

- What changes have occurred in the wider market that could be having an impact on your brands/products/services and how important are these changes to your performance?

- How is the brand/product/service performing relative to other markets/competitors/periods of time?

To answer the question:

  How will this data story create value for the business?

Try completing the following sentence:

  This data story will provide actionable insights and recommendations to help overcome [PRIORITY PROBLEM], in order to improve/optimize [SOURCE OF VALUE].

> For example:
>
> This data story will provide actionable insights and recommendations focused on the best marketing mix to help overcome the current budget constraints in order to reach the stretching goals of the acquisition strategy.
>
> This data story will provide actionable insights and recommendations focused on the new advertising copy recommendations to help overcome the negative customer perception around X, in order to improve overall loyalty and retention.

Step 3: Focus on a killer question

WHY CREATE A KILLER QUESTION?

Using one killer question for your data story can be a highly effective technique to create a compelling and focused narrative. The killer question:

- serves as a central theme, driving force or anchor for the entire story, guiding the data analysis
- enables you to identify some early hypotheses more easily
- frames the insights in a way that is meaningful and useful to the audience
- becomes a memorable hook that encapsulates the story essence
- forces you to exclude the superfluous, thus avoiding information overload
- avoids the complexity of having to manage multiple questions, resulting in disconnected data points
- sets the stage for a call to action – by virtue of asking a killer question your data story needs to offer an answer in reply

You have to be focused, because there's so much data, and if you try and boil the ocean, you're never going to get there. So you have to make sure that what you're delivering is something that's helping move the business forward. You're helping by saying this is working, this isn't working, this is what we need to do differently, here's what we're going to do to boost in the next quarter. It is not just about what your marketing strategy is; you have to do it in a way that's very closely aligned to the business strategy, because that's what marketing is there to serve.

Sinead Jefferies, SVP Customer Expertise, Zappi

HOW TO CREATE A GREAT KILLER QUESTION

A great killer question deserves some dedicated critical thinking to ensure we encapsulate what transformation we need to inspire, what matters most and why the story is important.

To create a great killer question you need to ensure it can:

- go beyond the objective
- hypothesize the answer

GO BEYOND THE OBJECTIVE

As highlighted in Figure 5.1, a great killer question requires three component parts:

1 **A specific objective that clarifies exactly what we need to know.** This can be subdivided into three different types of objective:

   a. an exploratory objective – a what, who, where and when question:

   i.   What has changed in the last quarter?

   ii. Where is the space/opportunity to differentiate?

   iii. What are the primary drivers of value?

   iv. What do the target audience like about the proposition?

   b. a discovery objective – a why question:

   i.   Why is this happening?

   ii. Why do prospective purchasers drop off at this stage of the journey?

   iii. Why are we failing to catch competitor X?

FIGURE 5.1 Three components of a killer question

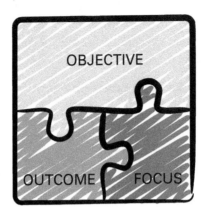

c. an action objective – a how question:

    i.   How do we fix/change/leverage/optimize/avoid…?

    ii. How do we enter markets successfully?

    iii. How do we continue to grow the brand?

    iv. How do we innovate to meet these needs?

2 **An end outcome that this objective will help us achieve and is viable to action.** This can be divided into either achieving a positive outcome or avoiding a negative outcome:

    a. a positive outcome – related to achieving our goals and targets with specific reference to the key performance indicator

    b. a negative outcome – related to avoiding further problems, losses or risks with specific reference to the key performance indicator

3 **A specific focus area that fits with key priorities.** This can be divided into three different focus areas:

    a. within a specific time/place – by a certain end point (this year, this quarter, etc.) or specific geography (country, region, etc.)

    b. within a specific target group – by segment, by demographic, by frequency of purchase, by channel usage

    c. within a specific set of criteria – within existing budget, within a benchmark, within a tolerance level

Example 1:

- Original question = Should we produce content on topic X?
- Killer question = *What is the appetite* to engage with topic X among our *loyal readers* and is this significant enough to have a positive *impact on advertising revenue* for the brand?

The original question covers the 'what we need to know' at a very broad level and will probably result in an answer that suggests 'it depends', with lots of analysis addressing pros and cons. It is missing any definition of what success would look like or parameters to make a decision on, making it hard to produce a data story from lots of potential data analysis.

The killer question provides greater clarity and depth by focusing on the three component parts:

1 The objective is to understand the size of the opportunity.
2 The outcome is the link to driving engagement metrics and advertising revenue opportunities.
3 The specific focus is existing loyal readers.

Example 2:

- Original question = How are consumers' shopping habits changing?
- Killer question = *What are the top three consumer shopping trends* that we need to plan for and respond to now to *stay relevant to segment A* and *gain share of wallet advantage over competitor X?*

The original is a real question posed by a category marketing team. It is far too broad and doesn't give any sense of priority actions that any analysis could support.

The killer question provides room for generating actionable insight by focusing on the three component parts:

1 The objective is to understand the priority shopper trends the brand should respond to.
2 The outcome is the link to gaining share of wallet over a specific competitor.
3 The specific focus is relevance for segment A.

Example 3:

- Original question = Why should we invest in paid social?
- Killer question = *What difference* would a *£x million paid social media investment* make to campaign X in terms of *mass market reach and ROI* compared to *other communications approaches?*

The original is a real question posed by a decision-maker who was sceptical about the need to include paid social in the communications budget. The question is too broad and doesn't give any room to evaluate the role of the channel in relation to specific campaign goals.

The killer question provides a tangible example and measure of success by focusing on the three component parts:

1 The objective is to understand the relative performance of paid social compared to other approaches.

2 The outcome is the impact on the campaign goal to reach a mass market audience in the most efficient way.

3 The specific focus is the £x million recommended spend.

Example 4:

- Original question = Are we attracting new customers to the brand?
- Killer question = Did the June campaign *targeted at 18- to 25-year-olds* result in an *increase in revenue for the new range?*

While this might be a common question, it is lacking in any specifics to create a compelling data story as it doesn't indicate what activity we are measuring, what new customers we are looking to attract or any measure of success.

The killer question provides an opportunity to evaluate what has worked by focusing on the three component parts:

1 The objective is to understand the performance of the campaign on acquisition.

2 The outcome is the impact on purchase of items within the new range.

3 The specific focus is the 18- to 25-year-old target market.

HYPOTHESIZE THE ANSWER

A killer question needs to strike a balance between not being too broad that the story becomes too generic, high-level and convoluted, and not so specific that the answer becomes a simple 'Yes', 'No' or 'It depends.' Equally, it needs to be stretching and challenging enough to enable new insights and a deeper understanding, but not so ambitious that it is impossible to answer.

To stress-test the killer question we can generate early hypotheses. To generate well-rounded hypotheses, you need to take into account the following questions:

- What do I expect the answer to the killer question to be and why?
- What do I hope the answer to be given our current plans, strategy and decisions and why?
- What evidence do I already have that supports the likelihood that this hypothesis will be proven to be true?
- What evidence would I need from any new analysis to suggest that this hypothesis is true?

In order to avoid unnecessary bias creeping into your chosen hypotheses, ask the additional following questions:

- Can I refer to an existing example or user case where this is true?
- What are the alternative hypotheses and why do I believe this one is more valid?
- What are the blind spots or existing assumptions that might be driving this hypothesis?

A perfect story plan with a perfect killer question and hypotheses is not necessary; what you are looking for is a solid start point. One hour of high-quality thinking will make a significant difference in the quality of your final data story.

Putting into practice

A key framework to assist you with planning your data story

Working with many business storytellers over the years, I have found the SCQA tool to be particularly useful. It is easy to understand and to apply in many contexts. When I run story planning sessions, such as the one described in the earlier case study, it is the SCQA that helps give structure to the workshop and keeps the brainstorm on track.

The SCQA tool is part of Minto's wider framework shared in *The Pyramid Principle: Logic in writing and thinking* (2021). It is a useful acronym to help you pull together your draft story plan, resulting in a clear and concise paragraph that forms the starting point for your story.

SCQA stands for situation, complication, question and answer.

- The *situation* is a one-or two-sentence summary of the status quo, wider context and how it aligns to the bigger picture.

- The *complication* is a one- or two-sentence summary articulating the problem statement.

- The *question* is our killer question that we have crafted from our understanding of the context.

- The *answer* is our hypothesis that is going to be the starting point for our analysis.

Example 1

Business A wanted to close the market share gap with its nearest competitor. One part of the marketing plan to support this was to make changes to the existing advertising copy to better promote the brand benefits. However, the marketing team had a number of challenges that would likely impact on success, including a reduction in the overall budget for advertising and an increase in competitor marketing activity.

The following SCQA was devised to provide a focused outline for the data story to highlight the impact of budget cuts on achieving the end goal. The hypotheses have been excluded to prevent sharing commercially sensitive information.

- *Situation:* To support the business goal of driving market share, we recommended developing new copy focused on leveraging point of differentiation A. This campaign is due to go live on date X.

- *Complication:* Our planned spend and activity for the campaign have been affected by the wider macroeconomic issues and budget cuts. This resulted in the decision to launch the new copy without any rigorous testing. Given uncertainty regarding the effectiveness of the copy changes, coupled with overall media spend cuts and aggressive competitor activity, we fear the new advertising will not protect market share.

- *Question:* How much impact has the aggressive action of competitor Y had on our brand equity and will our new advertising campaign and supporting marketing effort protect us from further erosion of share?

Example 2

Business B needed to quickly address revenue issues caused by the cost-of-living crisis to protect market share. While current rejuvenation plans were making some impact, the roll-out was slow and would not address all the immediate issues that the operation was facing. Marketing tactics were not as effective as those of the competition and immediate changes were required to remove friction for customers on promotions.

The following SCQA was devised by the marketing team to provide a focused outline for the data story to convince the board to buy in to changes to specific promotion mechanics, including the loyalty scheme. The hypotheses have been excluded to prevent sharing commercially sensitive information.

- *Situation:* Our primary focus is protecting and optimizing market share during a difficult trading period and a number of pillar plans have been put into place to support this strategy. Tough market conditions and competitor activity have had a significant impact on shopper perception and make for a more challenging environment to execute our plans.

- *Complication:* We cannot solely compete by driving value perception via discounting and our main competitor is closing the gap on our quality position, especially among repertoire shoppers. Customers are becoming increasingly savvy about shopping around and some of our promotional mechanics mean basket shoppers are at a disadvantage, causing them to have their heads turned and try elsewhere for top-up shops.

- *Question:* What are the priority marketing actions we need to take to overcome barriers to accessing deals in order to prevent customers switching to the competition?

Crafting your SCQA gives you a wireframe story that others can contribute to and co-create. Sharing your draft story ideas with interested parties, select audience members or team members enables you to seek clarification on priorities. Early input from others also ensures additional perspectives on hypotheses are built into any data analysis frameworks and facilitates initial challenges around myths, biases and expectations, rather than having to circumvent them at the delivery stage.

Challenge 1

Take an existing data story you have been involved with and reflect on the following questions:

- How well did the original data story frame the message by aligning to the moments that matter and specific goals and priorities?

- How well did the original data story highlight the scale of the issues and why this story is important to tell?

- How clear was the killer question in your original story? Was it implied or explicit?

- Given your evaluation, what would you have done differently at the planning stage to improve the relevance of the data story?

Challenge 2

Create a plan for a new data story using the techniques covered in this chapter. Remember to:

- Define the transformation that the story needs to inspire.
- Identify the commercial objectives that this data story supports.
- Evaluate the different pressures pertinent to the story.
- Create a killer question.
- Use the SCQA tool to pull together a one-page story plan.

KEY TAKE-OUTS

1 Defining the transformation you are looking to achieve will provide a clear focus for the data story.

2 Time spent planning will result in relevant data stories that align with what matters most with the audience.

3 Creating a killer question provides an anchor for our analysis that will help the development of the data story.

Coming up next...

In the next chapter we will develop a robust data story by using analytical skills to uncover relevant insights. It will provide ideas to help you access the right data solutions for your story, guidance on best practice data interpretation and a means to create actionable insights worth shouting about.

References

Minto, B (2021) *The Pyramid Principle: Logic in writing and thinking*, 3rd edn, Pearson Education, London

Schramm, J D (2020) *Communicate with Mastery: Speak with conviction and write for impact*, John Wiley & Sons, Nashville

6

How to discover a robust data story

In this chapter we will explore:
- the power of a robust data story
- the pitfalls to avoid when discovering your data story
- the three steps to best practice
  - access a range of high-quality data sources
  - question the data observations
  - draw out meaningful insight
- putting into practice

The power of a robust data story

QUICK RECAP

A robust story requires you to use your analytical skills to surface and discover key insights. Solid analysis and interpretation provide the opportunity for uncovering new insights and developing a richer, nuanced and credible data story.

Making a difference

The case study example below demonstrates the value of a robust data story.

CASE STUDY

Context

Team X were responsible for customer communications. This involved not only marketing communication, but all inbound and outbound communication with the customer. Part of their responsibility was to share customer feedback on communications and the impact on overall customer experience and churn. This required them to influence their colleagues outside of marketing in the wider operations without direct authority over their objectives and plans. As part of their usual ways of working, the team held a monthly meeting to share a key data story and agree any actions.

Challenge

Despite the source of data being valid, the team were constantly questioned about the robustness of the data story. If their stakeholders did not like the recommendations or actions in the data sources, they would default to criticizing the data itself. This defensive behaviour is something I have witnessed in many organizations, and while it is understandable that individuals may resist change or feel they do not have the tools or resources to implement change, it is easy to lose confidence in your data story if you feel the data is being unfairly scrutinized. The main challenge with the data storytelling was that the recommendations drawn from the data were not quick or easy fixes, nor were they particularly attractive or motivating to action. The stakeholders' feedback was that they were tired of hearing about these actions and wanted the data story to offer exciting new insight, not the same old recommendations. As the team dug deeper and deeper into the data, it didn't take long for them to realize that these mystical new insights didn't actually exist, and that their data interpretation would always prioritize the importance of the same three key actions, as these were the key drivers to improve customer communications.

Action

The team decided to change tack. Instead of mining for insights that were not robust or valid, they doubled down on the existing insights and reviewed their data storytelling approach.

No more time wasted on:

- creating visually appealing dashboards and presentations, using data that was at best ignored and at worst weaponized

- looking for phantom insights that didn't exist
- delivering awkward presentations that did not lead to improving the customer experience

Instead, they invested their time in developing a better data story centred around the three most important insights. This time allowed for:

- deeper data exploration across a broader range of sources
- collaboration with the finance team to develop models that could demonstrate the relationship between the insights and commercial KPIs
- reviewing recommendations and actions required against resources and capabilities
- adequately preparing for any challenging conversations that they would still face

Results

The team were able to come back to the stakeholders with the same insights from the data, told in a more powerful way, using robust data from multiple sources that aligned to an action plan. The work to validate the data story built their confidence in the recommendations and their ability to manage any scrutiny they might face. This confidence enabled them to be consistent in reinforcing the same message, until progress was finally made and a true transformation occurred.

Outcomes and learning

Buy-in to the data story helped make real change in communication activity and alleviate a number of customer pain points. The conscious, patient and robust data storytelling described in this case study highlights the significant impact insights can have on marketing and wider business outcomes. However, it also shows that, when the pressure is on, or we are busy, or we don't feel we have the right skills to influence with data stories, it is easy to succumb to any pressure to back down or change the story. Getting back to basics, being diligent in our approach and focusing on the robustness of the data interpretation can make a significant difference to great data storytelling.

The pitfalls to avoid when discovering your data story

There are three main pitfalls to avoid when discovering your data story:

- data distortion
- ignoring contradictory evidence
- failing to mitigate for bias in interpretation

Data distortion

Jerry Z Muller (2019) discusses the 'distortion of information' in his must-read book *The Tyranny of Metrics*. As the volume of data available increases, so too does the potential to manipulate and distort it. This distortion occurs day to day within our everyday lives and in our work. This can be magnified in teams and businesses that are looking to achieve ever more elusive short-term gains, and the marketing function is no exception. According to *Marketing Week*'s Language of Effectiveness Survey (Stephenson, 2023), 46 per cent of the 1,610 brand-side marketers interviewed felt that their brand is too focused on ROI at the expense of longer-term brand building. This pressure to prove ROI and short-term impact can lead to shortcuts when it comes to using data to drive marketing decisions and actions.

Sometimes, 'data distortion' is conscious and intentional. I have worked with well-respected marketing teams where they have been asked to prove certain claims to be true and have found themselves manipulating the data to do so. Some of the 'distortion' that happens in data storytelling is unconscious and driven by our innate human desire to simplify the complex into something that is more easily measurable. Examples of data distortion include:

- quoting declines in raw numbers, rather than as a percentage among the relevant base
- changing definitions or parameters to remove certain segments or categories within the data
- averaging quarterly data by three to make comparisons to monthly data when it was unavailable in certain markets

- measuring the impact of interventions based on the total numbers rather than the proportion of a variable base
- cherry-picking the data that proves the point that they need to make and ignoring any related data that does not
- encouraging, or turning a blind eye to, poor behaviours that game the metric

The reality is that it is possible to get data to say what you want if you look at it in a different way. While it might make someone happy in the moment or suit a specific agenda, it weakens any benefits to be had by using data in the first place. If we use data to prove that something worked when it didn't, then all we are doing is fooling ourselves. Eventually, the misuse of data catches up with us because the reality doesn't match what we have claimed to be true and the effectiveness we sought to demonstrate isn't realized.

Knowing how to use data ethically becomes everyone's responsibility when failing to do so can have severe legal, financial and reputational consequences. No customer is going to admire your brand for the great job you do at personalization if at a wider corporate level there is any question about misuse of data. Companies are penalized with significant fines for breaching data regulations. According to Data Privacy Manager (2023), the top fines imposed for breaching GDPR regulations in Europe in 2023 were €1.2 billion for Meta and €746 million for Amazon. In the UK, the Information Commissioner's Office has the power to fine companies that breach regulations up to £17.5 million or 4 per cent of the total annual worldwide turnover, whichever is higher.

Given these risks, it is crucial for marketing teams to prioritize data accuracy, solid analysis, ethical practices and robust data storytelling to effectively leverage data for strategic decision-making, campaign optimization and customer-centric marketing initiatives. As individuals within the marketing function, you need to use data as part of a persuasive storytelling approach that incorporates data in a conscious, robust and deliberate way.

Ignoring contradictory data

Managing contradictory data is an essential part of data analysis and can yield real insights if we embrace the mess and the discomfort it causes. Ignoring the contradiction can cause inaccuracy in interpretation and ultimately in decision-making. Given the data has been cleaned, validated and quality-checked by the data owner, we can be confident that the data is correct. If statistical testing has determined that the differences are significant, rather than just random variation, it requires the data storyteller to explain any differences and what they mean. Rather than ignore these differences, further exploration will be required to understand and make sense of the contradictions.

These contradictions could be due to:

- looking at data over different time periods or different samples – comparing apples with oranges
- looking at different types of measurement, such as attitudes versus behaviours – comparing apples with an elephant!

Often, the data wouldn't really match up because the sources of those data points could vary enormously. For example, data from a brand tracking study measuring awareness and perception of the brand and campaign is derived through an online survey (and therefore an online panel of 'non-rejectors' of the category), data showing advertising penetration is based on a completely different base and set of attributes, and social again is different. So, trying to pick out the stories in all of that was difficult. It's important to be aware of these differences and the limitations in order to make sense of all the information gathered and create a coherent understanding and evaluation of performance. It often took a lot of time to gather this data and analyse it, which often felt like we were on the back foot when it came to planning the next campaign as often the learnings from the previous one hadn't fully been understood.

Rosy Harrington, Global Brand Planner, De Beers Group

There are three steps to manage contradictory data to ensure it has a place in your data story:

1 Consult with others and seek input from subject matter experts to get a fresh perspective and help uncover potential explanations.

2 Incorporate insights into your data story as 'directional' only and review implications as new information becomes available. You can caveat these insights as 'watch and wait' while further data is collected that may resolve the contradiction.

3 When presenting your data story, be transparent about the presence of contradictory data and the steps you've taken to address it. Acknowledging uncertainty and imperfection is a sign of credibility and can help build trust in your analysis.

Failing to mitigate bias

Bias is normal, but trying to limit bias in data interpretation is crucial for making objective and reliable decisions from your data story.

Here are some of the key biases to watch out for in your interpretation:

- The 'not invented here' bias means it is easy for you to default to a sceptical or dismissive interpretation of data that comes from outside – whether that is from another team or external to the business. This can lead to a myopic interpretation of the data and can risk down-playing wider knowledge.

- Confirmation bias occurs when individuals tend to favour information that confirms their existing beliefs or hypotheses, while discounting or ignoring data that contradicts them. This can lead to cherry-picking data that suits your own agenda, rather than challenging your point of view.

- Cultural bias arises when differences or stereotypes influence the interpretation of data, leading to misinterpretation or misrepresentation of certain groups. This becomes more prevalent when you are removed from reality and exist within a marketing bubble.

- Anchoring bias happens when an initial piece of information has an undue influence on subsequent decisions or interpretations, leading to results that are biased towards the anchor. This could mean that early indications become the final interpretations, without you digging deeper or looking for alternatives.

The first strategy to minimize bias in your data interpretation is to acknowledge its existence. Everyone has biases – it is normal. The more transparent we can be about our process, our assumptions and areas of uncertainty, the easier it is for potential sources of bias to present themselves.

There are a number of additional ways of working that can also assist in minimizing the risk of bias:

1 Gather a range of different perspectives on relevant hypotheses at the planning stage.

2 Consider alternative explanations and look to disprove hypotheses when conducting your analysis.

3 Seek input from others and invite others to peer review our interpretation.

4 Replicate the findings through further research or experiments.

These are relevant tactics when looking at any datasets but are particularly relevant when looking at large datasets and using AI tools, as any bias can quickly be magnified and replicated at scale.

The three steps to best practice

1 Access a range of high-quality data sources.

2 Question the data observations.

3 Draw out meaningful insight.

In this section we will look at each in turn, why it matters and how to implement it in practice.

Step 1: Access a range of high-quality data sources

WHY HIGH-QUALITY DATA SOURCES MATTER

In Chapter 1 we explored Aristotle's *Art of Persuasion* and the need to balance ethos, logos and pathos in our data storytelling. Understanding the credibility of sources is imperative for executing ethos in our data storytelling practice. Using unreliable data can have serious consequences leading to flawed, incorrect or misleading data stories. This in turn may result in misallocation of resources, legal or compliance issues, or reputational damage with customers, partners and other suppliers. Using unreliable data can also lead to missed opportunities if we fail to accurately measure trends, emerging threats or changing customer preferences.

By selecting relevant, accurate and reliable data sources for our story we can be confident in the validity of our conclusions and recommendations. While you may not personally be responsible for data quality and governance, by understanding the data available to you and critically evaluating the source and methodologies you are taking accountability for the integrity of your own data story.

HOW TO ACCESS HIGH-QUALITY DATA SOURCES

To ensure you are using credible information sources that are accurate and trustworthy, you need to:

- find out what data sources are available
- speak to an expert or the data owner

FIND OUT WHAT DATA SOURCES ARE AVAILABLE

Before we can make any judgement regarding reliability, we need to understand which data sources are available on the topic area. Start with what you already have access to and review through the lens of your new killer question. It may be that existing sources can give you at least part if not most of the answer, without additional analysis. From this review you should be able to spot the knowledge gaps that still exist and make a judgement as to how critical they are to fill, before investing further time, resource and potentially budget acquiring more data.

While sticking to what you know can build trust in your interpretation, the downside is we may miss different perspectives or new insights. But when we don't know what is available, spending time investigating what else could be out there can be time consuming. I recommend focusing on uncovering other data sources that exist within the business or with trusted partners first. This is where great knowledge management systems can add real value, enabling you to access different sources that might sit outside your remit.

In the absence of a great knowledge management tool, lean on your network. But resist the urge to send an 'all staff' email requesting information. Instead, look to uncover new sources by sharing your story plan with other relevant peers, internal communities and trusted stakeholders. This way they can understand the bigger picture relating to your request for data, which will increase the likelihood of them being able to provide useful information. Requesting general information on a broad topic area is likely to mean that you become inundated with reports that may or may not be relevant to your investigation.

SPEAK TO AN EXPERT OR THE DATA OWNER

Understand the basics of the methods and techniques so you can collaborate with experts to find the best approach, rather than just asking for data science! For example, understand that prediction doesn't have to be machine learning and we can do a lot with advanced statistical techniques, or know when analytics can't help, and customer research would be better.

Rebecca Ruane, Head of Reader Revenue Insight, *The Guardian*

There are a number of questions to ask the expert or the data owner to help you make a judgement on the quality of the data source, including:

- Who is the author or owner of the data and are they an expert in the subject matter?

- Who is/was the intended audience?
- What is the purpose of the data source? Is it to inform or to sell?
- Who produced and paid for the data? Are they reputable, do they have their own agenda, or do we trust that they are impartial?
- Is the owner of the source independent or are there any known biases or conflicts of interest that can affect objectivity of the source?
- Is the platform where the data sources is hosted an established and reputable publisher known for credible content?
- Has the source been validated, peer reviewed or fact-checked?
- Is the source up to date?

Be curious about the source and how the data has been collected to ensure you are not opening yourself up to any risk by using the data. If the credibility of a source is unclear, seek advice from experts who can provide guidance on reputable sources for specific topics.

Step 2: Question the data observations

WHY QUESTIONING THE DATA MATTERS

> Before you as a marketer go off with numbers and use them or share them, you need to know that you can back them. You need to know where they came from. Don't be fobbed off by the black box or by someone telling you that you don't need to concern yourself with the detail. You need to be able to challenge everything about that number and own it.
>
> **Lizzie Harris, Customer Director, B&Q**

In 2020, Berlin artist Simon Weckert faked a traffic jam to make a point about the flaw in big data. As part of his project, and subsequent installation, 'Google Maps hack', Weckert used a small red wagon filled with 99 second-hand smartphones with the Google Maps app open. By walking around quiet city streets he created a signal cluster that indicated to Google Maps there was a traffic jam, therefore sharing data with app users that would impact on their decision-making around avoiding the route and seeking alternatives. By transforming a green route into a red one on the map he was highlighting the map's reliance on user data. This is a great visual example of how data manipulation can result in the communication of misinformation and how it can impact on decision-making.

Marketers do not need to know how to generate predictive models or run statistical tests (unless you really want to). It is not imperative to be a data expert to integrate analytical thinking into your marketing practice – it just requires a certain level of confidence when reviewing datasets, reports and presentations, plus the ability to ask good questions. Marketers may be reluctant to get their hands dirty with the data or have a fear of getting it wrong. This can lead to an over-reliance on the data expert for their interpretation of the evidence. Building confidence in our analytical skills requires demystifying the language around data, providing easy-to-replicate analytical processes and the empowerment to challenge the data.

HOW TO QUESTION THE DATA OBSERVATION

To be confident in the evidence that is informing your data story, you need to question the data itself. This requires the ability to look at the data and know what questions to ask to help you:

- check the findings are valid
- build confidence in your interpretation

CHECK THE FINDINGS ARE VALID

To test the validity of the data, there are a number of key questions you should ask:

- What is the sample and is it representative of the customers I am interested in?
- How recently was the data collected?

- Who is missing from this sample and what impact could that have?
- What is the margin of error on the sample size and what is a fair comparison?
- What are the sublevels/breakdown of results of any composite metric/KPI and how are they behaving?
- What is the range of scores that makes up the mean on any key measures?
- What are the key drivers of change in our KPIs and how strong are the correlations?

Asking these questions can elicit a great deal of insight, and with better quality analysis you will be better placed to make quality judgements on what course of action to take. Having sought answers to these questions you can now consider what the data means and your response to the killer question for your data story. Being confident enough to ask questions of the data will go a long way towards avoiding interpretation pitfalls and ensuring high-quality data interpretation and storytelling.

BUILD CONFIDENCE IN YOUR INTERPRETATION

Confidence comes not from knowing all the answers, but from being able to look at the data and know what questions to ask.

To get comfortable with data – get stuck in. Look at what's it telling us and how it is backed up with other credible sources. Be prepared to review the data at every stage. So, look at it early on, maybe at the 50 per cent stage, to see if any trends are emerging. And then check in again at 75 per cent and 100 per cent, just to see what the data is telling you and to see what trends and narratives are emerging. They may well change. It's important to keep on top of the data and just keep checking in on it. Don't just take it at face value and don't just wait until all the final data is in, because that's an opportunity for you to look at some secondary resources or other analysis and to be able to question it a little bit more.

Rachael Kinsella, Editorial and Content Director, iResearch Services

Some questions to ask yourself when looking at the data include those listed below:

Is the average meaningful?

For example, if customers are asked to rate a brand, they are likely to be given a scale to choose from. If that scale is 1–10 and the mean average in the data is 6 among a sample of 1,000 customers, what does this actually mean?

Averages are useful when conducting comparative analysis over time or between groups or markets, but as a tool to drive action they can be meaningless as they neglect the range of scores given that makes up that average. Looking beyond the mean to the range of scores can generate more insight than just the mean itself – it enables us to identify those that are positive and those that are negative and differences between their needs, attitudes and behaviours.

Is this uplift in the data significant?

Sample size, margin of error and confidence levels give an indication of accuracy in the conclusions drawn from the data.

For example, with a robust sample size of 1,000 responses or counts you could still have a margin of error of +/– 3 percentage points when comparing that data over time. Therefore, if the data for a particular measure has moved from 52 per cent, to 55 per cent, this uplift of 3 percentage points could be down to noise in the data rather than a real change. However, if it moved from 52 per cent to 60 per cent, this is outside the margin of error and so we could be 95 per cent confident that this is a real uplift.

It is important to know the sample size you are basing your decisions on, and with smaller samples or subsamples it is necessary to understand the impact of the margin of error when making comparisons over time or between groups. This might mean you need to look at a longer time period to ensure more stable data, or, if looking at a subsection of the data, look at the level above.

Can I be certain that making a particular change/intervention will lead to a positive uplift in a key measure?

Probability measures the chance of events occurring and whether results would be replicated if we conducted the same analysis again and again. If probability is 1 then it is certain to occur each time it was replicated; if probability is 0 then it is impossible it will occur ever again; and 0.5 is an even chance it could be replicated again – such as the toss of a coin. Understanding the difference between the possibility of something happening (e.g. it could technically happen) versus the probability of something happening (e.g. it will happen) is important when it comes to levels of certainty about future consumer behaviour based on current attitudes, forecasting and demand modelling. While you shouldn't expect a model to be based on a score of 1, as nothing is ever that certain, you should be asking more questions if it is less than 0.6.

Can I explain how a particular action/intervention impacted on the data?

Correlation measures the relationship between two variables to predict events. If the different variables are completely independent from each other and have no impact on each other the score is 0. If they are positively related, where if one improves the other does too, the maximum score is +1. If they are negatively related, where if one increases the other decreases, the minimum score is –1. Correlation analysis can provide information about different marketing metrics and their relationships with each other to identify key drivers that can be influenced through marketing and communications activity. Understanding the strength of that relationship will again impact on the level of certainty shared in your data story.

However, be mindful that correlation does not always imply causation. A strong correlation between sets of variables *might* indicate causality, but there could easily be other explanations, such as the result of random chance, where the variables appear to be related but there is no true underlying relationship or there may be a third, lurking variable that makes the relationship, appear stronger (or weaker) than it is. For example, although shark attacks and ice cream consumption are correlated, are they causally related? The per capita cheese consumption is correlated with the number of people who die from getting tangled in their bedsheets – but are these causally related? The key to check for causality is more questions and more experiments to test to see whether this relationship is consistent over time or in different settings.

Asking these questions might require you to build some basic knowledge of these key statistical terms, or you may prefer to just know enough to ask the relevant questions of the experts. Either way, it will help build your confidence in the conclusions you are drawing from the data.

> Get the language right. It's not just statistical significance – but also what do we mean by terms such as propensity or likelihood. You need to be able to understand and explain the data. For example, when you say the uplift is statistically significant, know what that means. You can then be more persuasive because you know the uplift isn't just a fluke.
>
> **Rebecca Ruane, Head of Reader Revenue Insight, *The Guardian***

Step 3: Draw out meaningful insight

WHY MEANINGFUL INSIGHTS MATTER

Meaningful insights hold greater significance than robust data observations as they provide actionable understanding. While data observations offer raw information or measurement of a metric, insights contextualize, interpret and extract valuable implications. Insights distil complexity, revealing patterns and relationships crucial for strategy refinement. They transform data into a strategic asset.

> Ask yourself 'Do we really understand the customer and their needs?' and 'Do we understand enough about our data landscape to be able to identify those needs at the right moment in time?' Data literacy is part of it but so is asking the 'Why?', understanding the 'So what?', being able to join the dots. Those are some very basic things that we all need to learn and get better at.
>
> **Sanica Menezes, Head of Customer Analytics, Aviva**

Example of a data observation:

> The cost-per-click (CPC) profitability metric for campaign X improved in March X.

Example of a meaningful insight:

> Although the CPC profitability metric for campaign X shows month-on-month improvement and was significantly better than our target in March, this was due to the fact that there was less competition, which lowered the CPC in that month, rather than because of any of the optimizations made.

HOW TO DRAW OUT MEANINGFUL INSIGHTS

To draw out meaningful insight from the data, you need to:

- dig deeper into the data
- interrogate the data for the 'So what?'

DIG DEEPER INTO THE DATA

Eyeballing the data in the spreadsheet, dashboard or report will give you a basic understanding of the data and you may be able to quickly answer some simple observations:

- Does this look right?
- Does it make sense?
- Is this interesting?
- Am I drawn to anything in particular?
- Are there any patterns/themes/trends I am noticing?

But to draw out meaningful insight you need to go beyond looking at the data at face value as it is unlikely that a quick review of the data will help you immediately answer your killer question. This will require a more detailed investigation to look deeper into the data with the killer question and hypotheses in mind.

When conducting your deeper-dive analysis, ask yourself:

- What metrics or measures are most helpful to me?
- How does the data compare to our hypotheses?
- How does it compare to past data, benchmarks or targets?
- How does this vary by segment, demographic or user type?
- How does this relate to the wider environment?
- How does it compare to other data observations I have seen?
- How does it contribute to a wider and deeper understanding of the problem or objective?

INTERROGATE THE DATA FOR THE 'SO WHAT?'

To understand why certain observations might be insightful, we need to interrogate why these changes or differences have occurred. By investigating the root cause, we are better placed to understand why the observation matters.

When conducting your root cause analysis, ask yourself the questions below:

- Why is this happening, and why now?
- What are all the directly relevant and connected factors?
- What factors or conditions contributed to these results?
- What are the most likely or probable reasons for this to occur?
- Have similar patterns/trends arisen in the past?
- Why does this matter more than other findings we have uncovered?
- How does it relate to what we are trying to achieve?

Asking the deeper root cause questions not only helps you build more thorough understanding of problems, drivers of change or potential solutions, it can also prevent recurrence of issues, improve optimization efforts and mitigate future risks.

Once your meaningful insight starts to develop, you can also utilize projective techniques and 'What if?' questions to scrutinize further. Below are a selection of questions you can ask yourself to ensure that you have considered the argument from as many perspectives as possible:

- If I shared this insight with [someone who often has a different or contentious point of view], what would they say and how would I defend this position?

- What could be a feasible alternative explanation and why is my interpretation better than any alternative interpretation? What evidence would convince me that the alternative interpretation is better?

- What if I am wrong? What would be the consequence, and would this stop me from pushing this message in my data story?

- What if I was the stakeholder in the audience? How would I feel or think about this data story?

- What if a customer was a fly on the wall? How would they expect the business to respond to this data story?

FIGURE 6.1   Example 5 whys

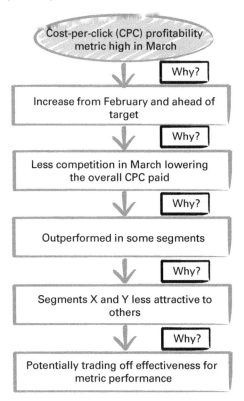

Putting into practice

A key framework to assist you with planning your data story

When running analysis sessions, I have found the 5 whys tool a quick and effective way of digging deeper into the data to surface meaningful insight (Figure 6.1). The 5 whys technique was invented in the 1930s by Sakichi Toyoda, the Japanese industrialist, founder of Toyota Industries and developer of lean manufacturing.

The 5 whys is essentially a problem-solving technique, and by iteratively asking 'Why?' it can help to identify the root cause of an issue. When faced with a problem, individuals or teams repeatedly ask 'Why?' to dig deeper into the layers of causation. Starting with the surface-level problem, each subsequent 'Why?' prompts a more profound examination, gradually unveiling the underlying causes. By the fifth iteration, practitioners typically reach a fundamental insight.

Challenge 1

Take an existing data story you have been involved with and evaluate the quality of the insight:

- How confident are you that the argument made in the data story stands up to scrutiny?

- In hindsight, what else might you have considered if you wanted to make the story stronger?

- Did the data story ultimately provide an answer to the question or just provide interesting findings?

- Did it highlight the root cause and provide a 'So what?'

- Given your evaluation, what would you do differently to improve the data story?

Challenge 2

Working on your story plan from Chapter 5, use the questions and techniques covered in this chapter to identify the credible data sources, analyse your data and identify the answer to the killer question.

Remember to:

- Ask questions of the data sources to ensure they are accurate and robust.

- Ask questions of the data itself to identify the relevant and useful findings that relate to your question.
- Ask the 5 whys to help you dig deeper and get to the root cause.
- Challenge your interpretation to make sure you have avoided the common pitfalls and can argue your case to others with confidence.
- Summarize your answer to the killer question.

KEY TAKE-OUTS

1 To maximize the value of your data story, use credible data from a range of sources.

2 Get comfortable asking questions about the data so you can own and trust your interpretation of the data story.

3 Keep asking questions to gain a deeper understanding of what story the data is telling you.

Coming up next...

In the next chapter we look at building a refined data story by using critical thinking skills to isolate the key messages for the narrative. It will provide ideas to help you synthesize and stress-test your insights into a coherent point of view, guidance on best practice story structure and a means to create a compelling narrative.

References

Data Privacy Manager (2023) 20 biggest GDPR fines so far, Data Privacy Manager, 19 September, dataprivacymanager.net/5-biggest-gdpr-fines-so-far-2020 (archived at https://perma.cc/S2B2-SMXQ)

Muller, J Z (2019) *The Tyranny of Metrics*, Princeton University Press, Princeton

Stephenson, J (2023) ROI top effectiveness metric demanded by C-suite, *Marketing Week*, 16 June, www.marketingweek.com/roi-top-metric-effectiveness (archived at https://perma.cc/6NQC-9RZV)

Weckert, S (2020) Google Maps hacks, Simon Weckert, simonweckert.com/googlemapshacks.html (archived at https://perma.cc/SRG5-NWET)

7

How to build a refined data story

In this chapter we will explore:

- the power of a refined data story
- the pitfalls to avoid when building your data story
- the three steps to best practice
  - o distil insights into points of view
  - o stress-test your recommendation
  - o weave insight into a compelling narrative
- putting into practice

The power of a refined data story

QUICK RECAP

A refined story requires you to engage your critical thinking skills to build the narrative. Distilling and stress-testing the insights to weave them together into a clear argument provides the opportunity to focus the audience's attention on the specific messages and asks.

Making a difference

The case study example below demonstrates the value of a refined data story.

CASE STUDY

Context

In late 2019 the brand director of a global financial services company instigated a strategic review of all customer feedback data sources and how they were communicated to the board. Data storytelling was seen as a key opportunity to drive more customer-centric decision-making from the very top, but existing outputs were under-performing. A few months into this review, and like many other organizations in early 2020, the operational delivery and customer service plans of the business drastically changed in response to the Covid-19 pandemic. This fast-tracked the need to reach senior decision-makers with better data stories, as it was imperative that they fully understood the immediate and long-term impact of these changes on customer perceptions towards their different brands. This now became a critical programme of work for the brand director, the head of customer experience and the insight partners from different business units.

Challenge

A number of challenges were identified by the team, including the following:

- Only highly sanitized data reports on customer experience were being shared with the board, with minimal insights on how to influence the globally mandated net promoter score (NPS) targets.

- The board were frustrated with the lack of joined-up thinking across the numerous data sources and wanted to see a greater link between the customer-led recommendations and the commercial value.

- Reporting was very transactional with limited 'So whats?' or 'Now whats?' for the individual brands that were operating in very different market contexts.

- Data was missing to explain the nuances behind the key drivers and granular data was not scalable to make the necessary inferences regarding the performance of specific actions and interventions.

It was clear to the team that current data storytelling was not fit for purpose and would require a significant overhaul if it was to provide more actionable insight and play a fundamental role in defining and driving customer strategy.

Action

To meet the need for immediate change, the team focused on working the existing data sources harder, conducting more deep dive analysis and synthesis across the different sources, developing a project management process to manage data storytelling, and improving the quality of the narrative within the existing mandated templates.

A proof-of-concept data story was built out from the data that already existed, as well as the new analysis and models that linked different attitudinal and behavioural sources. Working collaboratively in a small working group, the focus was on using the data to answer a killer question for each business unit that was relevant to their individual brands and markets, as well as developing an overall 'meta story' focused on the impact of the pandemic on customer expectations and relative brand performance.

Specific actions taken by the working group overseen by the brand director as the key sponsor of the programme of work included:

- a greater up-front investment in stakeholder conversations, hypothesis development and deep dive analysis sessions to draft the story and tie in specific activities

- a push to synthesize the different sources both qualitatively (using the story) and quantitatively, where correlations and comparisons were possible

- a shift in the focus of the board discussion paper towards the overall story coming out of the datasets, rather than reporting numbers in the scorecard

- a new format board report and personalized one-pagers for each of the brands that were designed around key customer journeys with commentary focused on areas of discussion in relation to their customer strategies

Result

While the change in the data story outputs led to more engagement with the board, it was the new ways of working that made the biggest difference to the quality of the data storytelling. Once the new data storytelling approach was embedded across the working group, it led to further enhancement of the data storytelling process, including:

- building data back in from the new models to the existing data sources to improve future analysis

- automation of standard analysis and reporting to free up more time for story building and communication
- creation of early warning systems to flag potential risks to core customer metrics

Outcome and learning

The changes that came about as part of the initiative required each of the individuals involved to think differently about their role as data storytellers. What resonated was the need to utilize collaborative ways of working to leverage their different knowledge, expertise and experience to develop a great data story. While additional time and energy was needed to invest in the new process, this was offset by greater efficiencies in standard reporting. The impact the changes had on the way senior management engaged with the data story was phenomenal and had a lasting impact on the value of customer metrics on decision-making at the very top of the organization. This case study shows the importance of refining the messages in the data story to move away from just explaining how various metrics are moving towards a customer-led narrative to drive real change in strategy.

The pitfalls to avoid when building your data story

There are three main pitfalls to avoid when building the structure of your data story:

- showing all your workings out
- not getting to the point
- wanting to avoid difficult conversations

We'll explore each of these in turn.

Showing all your workings out

When you get the opportunity to present your story, don't be tempted to show your workings out. Focus on the key messages and some simple takeaways. People don't need to see what is behind the scenes!

Charlotte Neal, Head of Marketing, Turning Point

When you are uncertain about your insights it is easy to fall into the trap of over-justifying them. This is especially true if the insights are challenging the norm, or the overall data story is negative. However, the reality is that beliefs are rarely changed by throwing more data at them! By showing all your workings out you are more likely to overwhelm and confuse the audience, rather than get them to understand and believe in your story. There is something credible in openly stating the main learning gained from your analysis and starting your data story with what you are recommending and why. Just because you are not showing all your workings does not mean that you haven't conducted robust analysis; you should be confident enough in your data story to consciously focus on the key messages only.

A recent presentation shared with me was a classic example of data storytelling style over substance. It took me too long to surface the key insights and recommendation from all of the data shared and I seriously doubted that the real audience would have had as much patience as I had. The purpose of the data story was to demonstrate how a marketing team in a global drinks brand could drive acquisition within a particular lifestyle segment and what that meant for their marketing plans, content and social media conversations. The data story was built from a rich mix of cultural analysis from ethnographic and other qualitative research, market sizing data, media consumption data, social media data and quantitative brand research. But the overall data storytelling had minimal impact because it failed to distil all of this evidence into an insightful narrative. In particular, the data story:

- demonstrated little to no connection to the brand strategy and why this segment was even important
- mistook a shopping list of interesting findings for a useful summary
- failed to deliver either a central recommendation or a prioritized set of actions
- followed a structure dictated by the different methodologies rather than a narrative structure
- reported on multiple occasions, mindsets, cultural codes, themes and motivations with no synthesis across these different measures,

making it impossible to understand what to prioritize in any marketing plan or specific campaign

- used multiple case studies collated in a section of the presentation, rather than illustratively weaved around any key point of view
- resulted in a 124-page report rammed full of visual social data, volumes of verbatim, streams of text commentary and complex coded diagrams that needed a number of charts to explain

While the quality of the data visualization was very good and the use of imagery used to bring the segment to life was powerful, the actual story was impenetrable because of the sheer volume of information, making it a perfect example of a data dump. All in all, this data story would have taken months to collect, curate and report, and required significant investment to produce, but there was very little insight and storytelling to show for it.

One of our expert marketers also shared an example from a recent meeting with CRM colleagues, stating:

> There is a balance to be struck around showing your proof points and adjusting them to the level that the audience needs to hear them. Rather than overwhelming them with an abundance of data that everybody just thinks 'Oh my God!', you need to be able to mine your data, make your point succinctly, use the data to underpin what you're saying and what you want to do, and then hit home your point, while pitching at a level that your audience can still follow.

Not getting to the point

Having sat through many thousands of presentations over the years, of which many hundreds failed to get to the point, one in particular stands out. Rather than tolerate the pain of a long-drawn-out data story like the rest of us, this senior stakeholder decided enough was enough and called it out. After the first five minutes, the data story-teller was still justifying the methodology used in his data analysis as a means to prove his credentials, when the commercial director inter-rupted and stated, 'I don't care how you did it and who you are – I am assuming I can trust you to have done what we have paid you for. I just need to know the answer to our ****ing question and what we need to do next.' It was a classic example of failing to understand the audience and their needs. Those working on the data storytelling had spent their time making their data charts look beautiful and providing an explanation that justified their work and their existence, rather than understanding why this mattered to the audience and what they needed to know from the data story. Distracted by his own safety net of the charts, the presenter had failed to get to the point. When this safety net was removed, the data storyteller struggled to get off the fence and provide a clear and logical answer to the killer question, causing further frustration and damaging trust in the story itself. Spending too much time on the output at the expense of understanding the core message has a detrimental effect on the impact of the data story.

The number one fear of getting to the point early among the delegates I have trained over the years is: 'If I tell them the answer up front, then why will they listen to the rest of the story?' They should really be thinking: 'If I don't get to the point early, why will they want to listen to the story?' This shows more concern for the attention 'payback' they are looking to achieve based on the time they have invested in the data story, rather than concern for whether the data story has delivered concrete value to the audience. All of our marketing experts focused on the need to be absolutely ruthless in getting the key message across, with one marketer calling out the temptation to sell in your work first. They stated, 'You may want to demonstrate all that work you've done, all the thinking that you've done, but actually the person receiving it doesn't care. As long as it answers their problem. But that's really hard to let go of.'

Wanting to avoid difficult conversations

Don't let uncertainty around the audience response and a fear of conflict dictate your approach. If there is bad news in your data story or a contentious point of view, there is no point trying to avoid it. You need to proactively manage it, rather than dilute, hide or sugar-coat it.

Putting your head in the sand risks leaving yourself exposed to scrutiny. Managing the difficult messages in your data story will mean you avoid awkward surprises, so look to get input from others before widening distribution and stress-test any contentious points of view with those who might be impacted. Use this early feedback to plan how best to position the story and prepare any additional analysis, content or conversations that will help you manage these challenges. I am personally a big fan of calling out the difficult messages up front and making sure the audience knows I understand this is going to be difficult or uncomfortable to hear. Being transparent about bad news or disappointing performance builds trust and credibility – avoiding, hiding or failing to acknowledge it can look duplicitous.

The three steps to best practice

1 Distil insights into a few salient points of view.

2 Stress-test your recommendation.

3 Weave together into a compelling narrative.

In this section we will look at each in turn, why it matters and how to implement in practice.

Step 1: Distil insights into a few salient points of view

WHY DISTILLATION MATTERS

In his paper 'The magical number seven, plus or minus two' (1956), George Miller detailed his law of human cognition and information processing, and his supposition that humans can effectively process no more than seven units, or chunks, of information, plus or minus two, at any given time. The premise is that when using short-term memory, humans struggle to retain and recall more than seven key points from a story. This means we need to identify the key messages we want our audience to focus on.

Miller also stressed the importance of recoding as a key component of how audiences process information. Recoding occurs as the brain reorganizes information into fewer units to help overcome the cognitive limitations of the seven-item processing limit. This natural distillation process is something you can duplicate when structuring your data story to reduce the cognitive effort required. Critical thinking skills are invaluable to ensure the fine balance between simplifying to aid recall and over-simplifying – this ensures that the value of the data story is maintained.

> We often sit through the big presentation by the market research agency with the client and we ask them questions and the agency uses slide after slide after slide after slide after slide. And at the end of it, we work with the client without the agency to help them distil that down to a single key overriding message, which is the same principle as you use with any advertising or communications campaign. It's really, really hard and we push the client to be really focused, but when you do it well and you give that part of the process effort you come out with something that is super-focused, extremely helpful to the creative process and easy for the audience to understand, leading to changes in their behaviour and opinions.
>
> **Lucy Davison, Founder and CEO, Keen as Mustard Marketing**

HOW TO DISTIL MULTIPLE INSIGHTS

To structure the data into a clear narrative you must first distil your insights. To build confidence in your distillation process you need to:

- recode to three to five points of view
- go back and answer the killer question

RECODE TO THREE TO FIVE POINTS OF VIEW

> You must boil it down to a couple of really salient points and ensure that people can see the connection and why that's important. It's the classic thing – and we've been talking about this for my whole 20 years in the industry. If you go in with a 100-slide deck, nobody's going to be interested. If you go in with two or three really compelling points that people can see are relevant, they are much more likely to do something. People don't know what to do when you give them too much information. Your job is to say 'We can see this is happening, and we know why, and this is what needs to change.' Focus on that and be really, really clear and that will get you so much more impact and will help unlock value.
>
> **Sinead Jefferies, SVP Customer Expertise, Zappi**

Here are some questions you might ask yourself to help recode:

- How can I group disparate learnings into *three to five* manageable themes that are easy to explain?
- What themes are critical to informing the recommendations in the data story?
- Why do these points of view matter more than other judgements or evaluations I could make from the data?
- How do I manage other topics of interest or hypotheses that do not align to the points of view and don't serve the story at this point in time?
- How can I articulate these points of view in a way that highlights their overall importance to the data story?
- How can I justify and support each of these points of view with the data I have analysed?
- What data is irrelevant/superfluous/repetitive and can be excluded from our data story, and why?

Once you have distilled your analysis into three, four or five themes then you need to craft these into solid points of view. Spending time crafting your points of view is critical as they are the key messages you want the audience to retain and retell from your data story.

Following these best practice principles will ensure you craft great points of view:

- It is important that each point of view supports the overall story and aligns to the killer question – it should feel like seamless reinforcement of the argument, not lots of disparate points nor unnecessary repetition.

- Each point of view can be related to the others but should be a distinctive point in its own right – they can be ordered chronologically (first, second, third), comparatively (best or most important to worst or least important) or structurally (a, b, c).

- A strong point of view avoids truisms and generalization to provide a unique perspective.

- A point of view should incorporate not only your learnings from the data (the 'What?') but also your experience and expertise to determine why this matters (the 'So what?') and what can be done about it (the 'Now what?').

- A point of view requires a short and succinct statement that incorporates verbs (such as optimize, inject, implement).

- A point of view should use conjunctions to enable connections between the 'What?' and the 'So what?' Garr Reynolds (2005) shares a simple framework that he discovered from Matt Stone and Trey Parker, the co-creators of *South Park*, where the conjunction 'and' is replaced with 'but' or 'therefore' to drive more tension into the point of view.

Some examples of a weak point of view

'Value is the issue on which we need to focus our engagement activities.'

This is too generic and could apply to lots of different data stories for many organizations. It doesn't outline what specifically about 'value' matters nor provide a reason why this should be the focus.

'We need to make the content relevant to issues they care about.'

This is an over-simplified truism that again applies to any marketing activity. It needs to provide specific reference to what the priority issues are and what that means for any new content or content changes.

'Our target shoppers are vulnerable to competitor discounts.'

This is purely an observation from the data rather than a point of view. While it may be true, it needs to detail what that means in practice and provide reference to actions to prevent this vulnerability.

Some examples of strong points of view

'Currently healthcare professionals have significant capacity issues that constrain the amount of time they can spend on device demonstrations or training, resulting in habitual prescribing based on their previous experience, which is a significant barrier to gaining trial and adoption of any new innovations such as product X.'

'The campaign was viewed very passively by the test audience, even if they were positive. What is considered as "pleasant" and "gentle" by some is viewed as "boring" and "dull" by others, so we need to inject elements into the creative execution that consumers can react to.'

'Proactive claim management, where customers feel that we anticipate their specific needs rather than respond to their chasing, is a key driver of advocacy in the category and one we need to improve if we are to reduce switching volumes to competitor X.'

'If we truly want to be seen as a company committed to providing for the health and wellness of all our customers, we need to implement programme X in our stores in lower income areas, as their profile suggests this is where the headroom exists to make the biggest immediate impact.'

'Someone's ability to quickly assess the quality of news underpins everything, and therefore if we want to reduce the risk of spreading fake news we need to consistently urge platforms to promote and highlight verified and fact-checked news content.'

'To drive subscriptions, we need to provide more space for our star content producers who rank highest on page views and reduce the number of articles of less than 750 words that do little to drive engagement.'

'Focusing the messaging on the unmet needs of "a high chance of winning", "transparency in how the game works" and "interesting bonus prizes" will give brand X a distinctive position when entering this saturated market.'

'Customers place considerable value on the support and stories shared by their peers, so brand X can leverage this by either partnering with advocacy groups or by signposting them to support resources that speak directly to the patient experience.'

GO BACK AND ANSWER THE KILLER QUESTION

Finally, you need to ladder up from your three to five key points of view to provide an overall answer to your killer question. This is your story resolution and the main message that you want the audience to take from your overall data story. This answer will help you resolve some, or all, of the conflicts, challenges and tensions in your story, and will help the business achieve its objectives and desired outcomes.

Questions you might ask yourselves when forming this judgement include the following:

- How does this answer build on, enhance or change our current plans?
- What is the benefit of this answer, and which specific tension will it help us overcome?
- What are the areas of compromise, and where are the red lines?
- What is the risk of doing nothing, doing what we always do or doing the wrong thing, versus taking the course of action we are recommending?
- What are the short-, medium- and long-term outcomes?

A great answer requires two components:

- It actually gives an answer to the question – no sitting on the fence!
- It encapsulates all of the points of view developed from your analysis.

To illustrate this with an example, I have taken one of the real killer questions shared in Chapter 5 and provided a fictitious response.

Killer question: What are the top three consumer shopping trends that we need to plan for and respond to now to stay relevant to segment A and gain share of wallet advantage over competitor X?

Answer: The three trends we need to respond to this year are 1, 2 and 3, with 1 offering the biggest opportunity for us to steal share of wallet. The criteria we used to judge each trend for relevance to this segment were X, Y and Z as they align most closely with the core brand position.

POV 1: Trend 1 outperformed all other trends on all three key criteria, therefore making it the obvious choice for us to focus on, but we will need to leverage our existing strengths in strength A and strength B if we are to be considered authentic in this space.

POV 2: To make the most of the opportunity to increase relevance with segment A we need to reinforce our key points of differentiation from competitor X by specifically dialling up our messaging around …

POV 3: While trend 4 did perform well on criterion X and is being talked about a lot in the business now as being an obvious choice to address X, this will be a distraction to optimizing relevance with segment A because …

Step 2: Stress-test your recommendation

WHY STRESS-TESTING MATTERS

Stress-testing our recommendations to ensure they are practical is a critical step in any decision-making process. Team members and stakeholders are more likely to commit to and engage in initiatives that they believe are feasible and have a realistic chance of success. By evaluating the practicality of the insights, we increase the likelihood of tangible results and enable future-proofing of any decisions and actions.

HOW TO STRESS-TEST YOUR DATA STORY

To build confidence in the narrative and stress-test your recommendation you need to:

- review desirability against feasibility
- assess commercial viability

REVIEW DESIRABILITY AGAINST FEASIBILITY

To determine whether a recommendation will be practical and lead to clear actions, there are a number of questions for you to consider:

- Will the recommendation lead to *desirable* decisions and actions?
  - Is this initiative or optimization likely to be successful if implemented?
  - Does the evidence suggest customers see value in the idea/change/creative?
  - How does this idea/change/creative fit with the priorities and needs of the customer?
  - Is this something our competitors have done?
  - Is there demand in the market that means we will lose out if we do not implement it?
  - How big is the opportunity?
  - How does it compare to other ideas/changes/creatives we have implemented in the past?
  - Is the market ready for it?
  - Do we have any predictive analysis to quantify the potential impact?
  - What is the risk of doing nothing, or doing something else instead?
  - What factors are critical to success that we will have to meet?

- Is the recommendation *feasible* to put into practice?
  - Do we have the resources/knowledge/experience/expertise?
  - Do we have the time, given other priorities?
  - Do we have the technology or operational capabilities to support this?
  - Are we legally allowed to do it?
  - Does anything else like this exist?
  - Have we considered the 'go to market' changes required?

In an ideal world you will be looking for a solution where there is demand and desire that is also feasible to implement. However, there may also be new opportunities to explore and conversations to be had, even if there is an imbalance between the two. For example, in a case study for a fast-moving consumer goods (FMCG) brand marketing team, the data story identified a significant demand for a new product variant to meet the needs of the consumer that would also support the long-term strategy to protect their number one status in the category through new innovations. However, from a practical perspective, the organization was not equipped operationally to produce the packaging format needed for this product variant. Instead of coming up with an easier incremental action, the team stayed true to their data story but positioned the message around the size of the opportunity and the art of the possible. The data story led to a partnership with an external packaging supplier that was eventually bought out by the organization once the new variant proved to be commercially successful.

ASSESS COMMERCIAL VIABILITY

Just because an action is attractive and you can do something about it doesn't mean you should. You need to remain true to the overall strategy and priorities, as well as ensure the action is commercially viable. To stress-test the data story and determine whether the recommendation will result in commercially viable actions there are a number of questions for you to consider:

- Is the recommendation commercially viable and worth pursuing?
- Are we going to make enough revenue to justify any investment cost?
- What is the opportunity cost of focusing on this versus other priorities?
- Will it damage our reputation if we get it wrong/it doesn't work?
- Is it of strategic benefit, even if not commercially beneficial?
- Is it scalable?

FIGURE 7.1 The data story sweet spot

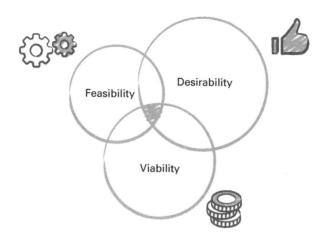

- Is there a long-term market for this?
- Why now? Why not wait and see?

Although the sweet spot identified in Figure 7.1 would be ideal, we may not have all the answers in our data story to make that judgement. If our resolution is desirable and feasible, we may have to run a trial or test before we can make a judgement on commercial viability.

For example, a brand team is concerned that analysis is indicating a potential reputational risk by continuing to invest in a social media platform. Other brands have chosen to step away from the platform and the team are questioning whether they should cease activity and switch advertising budgets to other platforms. However, further analysis shows that the majority of their loyal customers do not have a particularly strong opinion about brand fit with the platform and commercially the return on investment remains consistent. Given that there are likely to be some constraints in switching, the data story takes the position that the brand should implement a 'watch and wait' policy, but keep an eye out for any change in customer perceptions that might require a different approach further into the year.

By asking these questions of your data story you will be better placed to position priority actions and recommendations and deal with any areas where the data story might be challenged.

Step 3: Weave together into a compelling narrative

WHY NARRATIVE STRUCTURE MATTERS

Humans are naturally drawn to narrative structure due to its inherent ability to engage emotions, simplify complex information and enhance understanding. It provides the framework that our brains find easy to process, and by offering a journey with a beginning, middle and end it satisfies our cognitive need for coherence. Narratives tap into the way our brains naturally process information, making them a crucial component of data storytelling.

> I have a very simple approach to data storytelling, which I often do myself and encourage the team to do to avoid getting caught up in the data. I try to get them to pull away from the data, leave it behind, and get them to just tell me what are the big things that are coming out of the data. Quite often, they can articulate the story much better than they think. Then I tell them to just write down what you've just said to me, in five bullet points – like the elevator pitch. Simplifying it to that is really hard for people because they have all this information, and they feel that they've got to tell the audience about all this information. The key strength is being able to just say 'This is what it's telling us. Sure, there's loads of bits of information that I can add in afterwards. But this is what we're trying to tell you.' And then it's much easier to tell the story.
>
> **Richard Colwell, CEO, Red C Research & Marketing Group**

But the real magic of narrative is its use of tension. As John le Carré is oft quoted as saying from his interview with the *New York Times* (Barber, 1977), '"The cat sat on the mat" is not a story. "The cat sat on the dog's mat" *is* a story.' Bringing in an element of tension, you move your data story on from sharing observations to utilizing story mechanics that actively connect with the audience's brain. Instead of passively processing a fact or data observation such as 'The cat sat on the mat', the use of tension actively engages the brain through stirring curiosity and prompting questions, such as 'Why is the cat sitting on the dog's mat?' or 'What might happen if the dog comes into the room and notices where the cat is sitting?' It even enables the brain to paint a visual picture that connects with the narrative and projects forward to potential future scenarios without having to use explicit words to explain. This is how to connect your audience to the data story – give them a tension to think about before resolving it with your data-driven recommendations.

HOW TO WEAVE A NARRATIVE FOR YOUR DATA STORY
To weave a narrative that pulls together all the components from your planning, analysis and interpretation you need to:

- follow a storytelling framework
- ruthlessly edit for clarity

FOLLOW A STORYTELLING FRAMEWORK
In Chapter 5 we introduced the SCQA tools from the Pyramid Principle framework (Minto, 2021) as a means to develop your story outline. In this chapter we will revisit the tool as a useful framework for pulling together all the story strands into a well-structured narrative. While there are other frameworks that exist, I have found the Pyramid Principle to be best placed when creating a data story as it helps manage all the detail and helps the data storyteller balance a succinct story with using the most compelling evidence.

Like many storytelling frameworks, the SCQA approach aligns with 19th-century scholar Gustav Freytag's dramatic arc (Boyd et al, 2020) and leverages the strengths of universal storytelling. Figure 7.2 maps how the two overlap to build confidence and extra validity in the SCQA tool.

- Freytag argued that the upfront exposition sets the scene by sharing relative context, which aligns with the situation in Minto's SCQA.
- In Freytag's arc the focal part of the story is the central conflict or tension that must be grappled with, which aligns with the complication in Minto's SCQA.

FIGURE 7.2   The overlap between SCQA and Freytag's dramatic arc

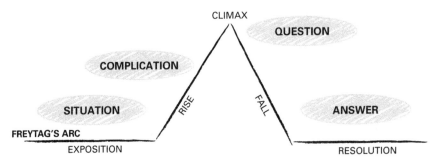

- Freytag's arc peaks at the top of the narrative arc at the story's climax where the tension leads to a decision that leads to a resolution, which aligns with the question and answer components in Minto's SCQA.

Minto's Pyramid Principle expands beyond the SCQA to reveal how the points of view and the selective data can be used to justify the answer. The pyramid structure uses a chunking approach – this is a cognitive process where information is managed in chunks, making it easier for the audience to process and remember. Each chunk in the data story is held together by the key point of view and the supporting data for that point of view. This framework therefore helps with balancing the overall story, the supporting messages and the evidence in the data story. Figure 7.3 shows the structure of a data story using the Pyramid Principle approach.

RUTHLESSLY EDIT FOR CLARITY

Once you have structured your narrative using the framework, it is time to ruthlessly edit to avoid overload. This is an essential step to maintain the quality of the narrative. Use your killer question as an anchor to make the decision about what stays in and what is left out of the data story. And when you think you are done, have one final check to make sure the data story is as fine-tuned as it possibly can be.

FIGURE 7.3   An illustrative example of a story pyramid

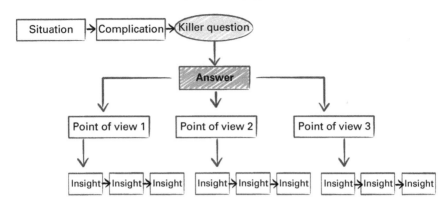

Editing takes practice – it takes us out of our comfort zone. But most of your audience will be used to consuming content that has been managed for the different levels of time and attention they have. And they will expect nothing else from your data story. So, seek inspiration from the news media, journalists and content producers who excel at this skill. Try practising editing your data story to create:

- a one-page summary for a five-minute read
- one or two paragraphs for a two-minute read
- a 30-second soundbite
- a Tweet

Putting into practice

Challenge 1

Take an existing data story output that you are familiar with and audit it for best practice:

- Did the output have a balanced beginning, middle and end, or did the detail in the middle dominate?

- Did the story flow effortlessly, or were there parts that jarred?
- How confident are you that the argument made in the data story stands out?
- Did the story use tension to draw you in?
- Did the story resolve the tension?
- Was the detailed data chunked into easy-to-consume sections?
- Did the data included in the output clearly align with the narrative structure or was there superfluous data that could have been moved to an appendix or another mechanism for reporting?
- In hindsight, what else might you have considered if you wanted to make the story stronger?
- Given your evaluation, what would you do differently to improve the data story?

Challenge 2

For your revised data story that you have defined and developed in Chapters 5 and 6, use the principles and techniques covered in this chapter to develop your narrative structure.

Remember to:

- Use the SCQA and Pyramid Principle framework to help you with the flow and balance between narrative and data.
- Perfect the tension within your points of view to draw your audience into your story.
- Challenge your use of evidence and ruthlessly edit to ensure that only what is necessary is included.

KEY TAKE-OUTS

1 By distilling your insights into three to five points of view, you help reduce the cognitive load on the audience.

2 Stress-testing your recommendations for desirability, feasibility and viability ensures your data story is actionable.

3 Using a framework to help define the narrative ensures your data story utilizes tried and tested story mechanics.

Coming up next...

In the next chapter we look at creating a relatable data story by enriching the data-driven narrative with human experience and real-world examples. It will provide ideas to help you bring your data story to life, to drive engagement and connection with the audience.

References

Barber, M (1977) John le Carré: An interrogation, *New York Times*, 25 September, archive.nytimes.com/www.nytimes.com/books/99/03/21/specials/lecarre-interrogation.html (archived at https://perma.cc/33BR-QM7M)

Boyd, R, Blackburn, K and Pennebaker, J (2020) The narrative arc: Revealing core narrative structures through text analysis, *Science Advances*, 6 (32), www.science.org/doi/10.1126/sciadv.aba2196 (archived at https://perma.cc/A7WZ-SSE9)

Miller, G A (1956) The magical number seven, plus or minus two: Some limits on our capacity for processing information, *Psychological Review*, 63 (2), 81–97

Minto, B (2021) *The Pyramid Principle: Logic in writing and thinking*, 3rd edn, Pearson Education, London

Reynolds, G (2005) The key to story structure in two words: Therefore and but, Presentation Zen, 22 May, www.presentationzen.com/presentationzen/2015/05/the-key-to-story-structure-in-two-words-therefore-but.html (archived at https://perma.cc/PC9J-GJG4)

8

How to create a relatable data story

In this chapter we will explore:

- the power of a relatable data story
- the pitfalls to avoid when creating your data story
- the three steps to best practice

  o integrate human experience and real-world examples

  o add the personal touch

  o keep the momentum going

- putting into practice

The power of a relatable data story

QUICK RECAP

A relatable story requires you to use your emotional intelligence to create a holistic data story. Enriching the data story with human experience and grounding it in real life increases the likelihood that it will cut through, resonate and influence your audience.

Making a difference

The following case study demonstrates the value of a relatable data story.

CASE STUDY

Context

This data story example was investigating the growth opportunities for a drinks category. The marketing team were looking to develop customer-led innovations and reposition several brands in their portfolio to tap into opportunities in this category. The data story needed to educate senior decision-makers within each brand and external communications partners to convince them of the need to instigate a change in direction. The data story was based on multiple sources, including expert interviews, social listening, market data, audience data, three years' worth of performance data and a global usage and attitudes research study.

Challenge

The team faced a number of challenges with creating the data story:

- The category is relatively traditional in comparison to others in the sector and, while innovations have cut through and helped drive revenue in the past, they have typically been 'me-too changes' taken from following trends and ideas from adjacent categories, rather than forging their own path.

- The volume of data and potential routes forward coming out of the analysis could easily confuse and overwhelm the different audiences or result in multiple different actions across the brands and markets. Like similar data stories exploring trends and segments, it had the potential to become an unwieldy 120-page data dump.

- The audience were very different to the consumer profiles that the data story was recommending as new targets and there was a potential for disconnect and lack of empathy.

Action

The priority focus was on creating a strong data storyboard that could be integrated and built upon through conversations with relevant stakeholders before finalizing recommendations that would be shared with the brand directors and category leaders in key markets.

Results

- The finalized data story incorporated a hook that focused on a landscape analogy using mountains, maps and pathways to highlight distinctive routes that consumers could navigate based on preferences and occasions – this hook was brought to life with real human examples and was used as a reference point throughout the story and as an anchor for managing the nuances in the data.

- The story context was shared in a visual summary and included a killer question that would serve as a focal point for the story – this simple use of the SCQA approach discussed in Chapters 5 and 7 helped frame the parameters for what the data story would and would not explore.

- The high-impact start also included the answer to the question upfront, giving the audience the high-level version of the story before delving into the detailed data story.

- A visual summary of the nine potential growth areas was synthesized and recoded into three simple subcomponents of growth – more people, more often, higher price – thus structuring the data story into three bite-sized and meaningful chunks.

- The growth routes served as the key points of view for the structure of the story and each section included a summary of the point of view, including an estimate of volume or value impact, the pathways to growth and the stress-tested recommendations to activate.

- Despite there being nine key areas to investigate in the detailed data story, each section was consistent in format and structure, making them easy to navigate through the detail.

- Each of the nine sections was summarized at the end with what, why, when, where and how, as well as some thought-starter questions to generate further thinking.

- The data visualizations were ultra-simple and consistent. Insights were synthesized across the multiple sources using very simple diagrams to show the meaning and take-outs

- Imagery and verbatims were used selectively to illustrate key points of view, rather than becoming an overwhelming data source in their own right.

- The ending focused attention back onto the mountain analogy with three key questions for the audience, as well as a quote from an industry expert on how this category has failed to capture trends in the past and a provocative statement to encourage action.

Outcomes and learning

The data story served as a great enabler for thought-provoking conversations with different stakeholder audiences and was used and referenced extensively in developing the brand strategies and in category conversations with retail buyers. By using a clear narrative structure alongside human experience, metaphor and personalized recommendations, the data story was able to connect, influence and persuade. The story output was bespoke to the specific context, challenge and data. Although this meant it required significant effort to craft into a meaningful data story, the level of impact it therefore had was significant.

The pitfalls to avoid when creating your data story

There are two main pitfalls to avoid when creating your data story:

- defaulting to the tools and existing templates
- forgetting your audience are humans too

Defaulting to tools and existing templates

It is easy to stick to the prescribed templates from previous data story outputs or the standard output produced by any tools you use for data analysis. But these default practices can limit our ability to reach and influence others, as they do not encourage us to engage with our creative brain to work out the best way to tell the specific data story for the specific audience.

Many data visualization tools and data storytelling platforms are primarily designed for reporting purposes and leave little space for bespoke data storytelling. Dashboards are useful tools for reporting comparative data for key metrics and help distribute the mental workload required to interpret meaning. Effective data storytelling tools used well can help to filter out the noise and assist the user to recognize patterns, spot exceptions and focus in on the key signals coming from the data. While these tools can make the analysis and interpretation process easier, they cannot – in themselves – create a data story that can be used to influence others. For marketers looking to create persuasive data stories, these data visualization tools and dashboard reports are enablers and inputs, not the final output. A significant amount of work and consideration needs to be made outside of the tool.

Templates for your story outputs can reduce the time taken to create your data story and draw on a consistent format, structure and style. But relying heavily on a template can produce generic data story outputs that look like every other presentation that your audience has seen that week. Predetermined structures and visuals can be restrictive and may force you to align your data story output with a prescribed way of presenting the data. Allowing a degree of customization is going to be critical when it comes to telling your data story. If templates are mandated, you will have to find a workaround and think creatively about how to use the space on the prescribed template to get the story message across. If you have more freedom you can incorporate different tools and approaches to help bring the story to life.

Forgetting your audience are humans too

It is easy to think, once you have a well structured narrative supported by robust evidence, that the story will tell itself. If you were communicating with robots then maybe that would be the case, but, assuming your audience are still humans, you need more than data and logic to cut through, reach, influence and persuade. Even the most powerful statistics can fall on deaf ears if they are not positioned in a way that connects with the audience. Make sure you give time and effort to thinking about the story mechanics that instigate an emotional connection.

One of the lasting memories of my early career in leisure retail is a data story that resulted in the data storyteller being removed from the meeting by a senior stakeholder. The data story was focused on early-stage customer insights gathered on a new retail proposition we were testing for potential roll-out. The evidence had been gathered through in situ quantitative interviews with paid customers on entry to and exit from the venue, researcher observations and ethnographic studies, where the target market were recruited for an accompanied night out at a number of venues, including the test site. Rich with both qualitative and quantitative data sources, the story highlighted several insights to optimize the final proposition and had the potential to be a highly immersive data story.

However, the agency partner responsible for creating the data story made the decision to send a senior director who had zero involvement with the project to present the data story, with the false belief he would have more credibility with the senior audience than the junior researcher who had conducted all the qualitative fieldwork and analysed the data. Given his lack of familiarity with the project, all the data storyteller could do was read out the presentation to the audience. He was unable to add any examples or nuance from his own observations, provide any anecdotes from interactions with the customer in the venue or answer any questions that required him to share his personal perspective or point of view. These stories would have brought flavour and depth to the story and given the audience a stronger understanding of the response to the proposition by the target market than any bar chart or verbatim comment ever could. He had no real understanding of the data story himself and he was only able to communicate what was in the deck of slides that someone else had created for him. The audience were frustrated with the data story from the beginning, which led to more questions and even greater exposure. When quizzed again on his own point of view and having revealed that he had in fact never been to any of the test sites, let alone conducted any of the fieldwork himself, he was asked to leave and for the junior researcher to take over. Despite the junior researcher doing a brilliant job and being able to bring the data story to life, a lot of damage had been done and a lot of work behind the scenes was required to rebuild faith in the insights as part of the roll-out decision-making process.

This example demonstrates that credibility is not just about having robust data shared in a coherent structure – it also means having a credible storyteller who can share the story in a believable way to fellow humans!

The three steps to best practice

1 Integrate human experience and real-world examples.

2 Add the personal touch.

3 Keep the momentum going.

In this section we will look at each in turn, why it matters and how to implement in practice.

Step 1: Integrate human experience and real-world examples

WHY HUMAN EXPERIENCES AND REAL-WORLD EXAMPLES MATTER

In Chapter 1 we explored Aristotle's *Art of Persuasion* and the need to balance ethos, logos and pathos in our data storytelling. Given humans are not motivated by logic and evidence alone, you need pathos to drive an emotional connection with the data story that will move the audience to think, feel and act. Pathos means bringing the data to life using human examples of real experiences or journeys and grounding abstract data concepts into everyday practices that are easily understood. By evoking emotion in the audience, you give them a reason to care about the data story. By simplifying complex data and making it more accessible, you make it easier to understand and to engage with.

Humans can express empathy for another individual human through hearing their story but cannot connect in the same way to a statistic or a set of data points. You need to weigh up the advantage of storytelling as a means to engage, connect and influence alongside the risk of any narrative bias and misinterpretation. Dahlstrom (2021) argues that narratives can play a powerful role in combating scientific misinformation, and his article 'The narrative truth about scientific misinformation' explores the tension surrounding the role of storytelling in both the creation and the dissemination of scientific misinformation. Despite the evidence suggesting the risk that audiences find it hard to distinguish facts from falsehoods within a story, he also determined from the research that stories have more influence on attitudes and behaviours when compared with data and information. As part of this study, he concluded that 'the underlying purposes of both science and narrative are not that different. They both seek to make sense of the world and find our place within it. By bridging the two, narrative can also help science counter misinformation by providing meaning to reality that incorporates accurate science knowledge into human experience.' Specifically, the research concludes that, although the use of story mechanics can be a cause of scientific misinformation, it can also be the remedy, depending on how well the narrator marries the evidence with story in the narrative.

This need to balance the substance of the data with the benefits of the narrative is also referenced by Lydia Hooper, designer, facilitator and author. In her article 'Ten ways cognitive biases impact data design work' (2020), she concludes that 'stories are best when they balance both statistical trends and the experience of real people'.

HOW TO INTEGRATE HUMAN EXPERIENCE AND REAL-WORLD EXAMPLES
To ensure you are integrating experiences and examples in a way that adds to the value of the data story and retains integrity, you need to:

- utilize qualitative data
- incorporate a story hook

UTILIZE QUALITATIVE DATA
Tapping into qualitative sources can bring richer experiences into your data story, as well as provide you with relatable examples to bring the data to life.

Examples of qualitative enrichment include:

- customer interviews to add depth and context
- first-person narratives to provide nuanced insights into customer experiences and motivations
- customer observations to reveal pain points, preferences and emotional responses

Utilizing qualitative data can generate a more holistic and human-centred understanding that enhances the impact of data-driven narratives. Review existing qualitative sources through the lens of your specific data story or seek new qualitative sources to bring the human back to the centre of the story.

A well-constructed human story gathered from qualitative sources can prepare the audience for the main content of the data story, making it easier for them to absorb and understand it. Priming with a human story enables your audience to process the story on a simple, human and emotional level before they connect with the logical data story. It helps them to connect the information to an idea that is already understood in the brain. Reinforcing the human story over time to nudge the audience to take action is a good shortcut to help them recall the data story without having to repeat key messages over and over again.

INCORPORATE A STORY HOOK

The importance of a good hook is rooted in both cognitive psychology and effective communication principles. According to John Medina, a molecular biologist at the University of Washington, you have just under 10 minutes to keep your audience's attention (Gallo, 2018). Medina's studies show that our brains are wired to a primitive timing mechanism, and after 10 minutes your audience's attention will plummet. It is therefore imperative to hook your audience early and cover your main messages from your data story in that first 10 minutes. Given human attention spans are limited and your audience are being bombarded with data and content on a daily basis, we need to quickly cut through the noise in their heads, capture their attention and give them a reason to keep listening to or reading the data story. If you don't have them engaged early on, then they will not stay with you and all the great data analysis you have done will be wasted.

Your story hook should be both audience-centric and in service of your data story and is a great way to inject an emotional connection. This is not about being gimmicky for the sake of attracting attention; it is about leveraging a hook to ensure that the audience connect with the data story and consider the key insight messages and recommendations.

There are a number of different ideas for hooks that can build an emotional connection and ensure your data story is relatable:

- an individual story that connects with the human experience
- a killer stat that puts the story into larger perspective
- a metaphor that translates a complex challenge into an everyday decision
- a future scenario that highlights what is possible

A human story

Using human stories taps into a natural affinity for understanding others and the challenges and dilemmas they face. They enable the audience to connect with the real people behind the data, making the data itself more relatable. It helps to explain why the data story matters and how it impacts real life, fostering empathy, allowing us to vicariously experience their struggles and triumphs, and reminding us of the real-world implications of our decisions and actions on real people. Done well, it can lead to a biochemical response in the audience where oxytocin levels surge, giving the audience a vested interest in finding out what happens next or finding a way to improve the situation. In a ground-breaking study, Paul Zak (2014), Founding Director of the Center for Neuroeconomics Studies, Professor of Economics, Psychology and Management at Claremont Graduate University, and the CEO of Immersion Neuroscience, investigated the neurobiology of storytelling to see whether it could be used to 'hack' the oxytocin system to motivate people to engage in cooperative behaviours. The study discovered that character-based stories with emotional content aid understanding, recall and impact.

A human story works well as a hook:

- when we want the audience to consider different or alternative perspectives and experiences to their own
- where there is a disconnect between business decisions and the impact on the customer
- where we want to communicate a journey or lived experience

Individual stories work best when seen as an authentic voice, rather than filtered through the lens of the narrator. Telling the true, raw story of a real person will always make a greater impact on the audience than a polished version of their experience. While the aim is not necessarily to make your audience cry, I have seen boards moved to tears when listening to a first-person account of real experiences an individual has had with their brand and the impact that has had – positive or negative – on their life.

Human stories can also serve as anchor points for the data. By presenting a story at the beginning as your hook you can create an interesting reference point that the audience can return to as they navigate the data, helping them stay oriented, or even use the individual in the story to act as an alternative narrator. However, human stories can raise ethical considerations related to data use and privacy, so we need to ensure we have permission when using a personal story.

Human stories that you could use in your data storytelling include:

- your own personal story as a consumer or customer
- a strong verbatim showcasing positive or negative sentiment from a customer
- a hypothetical user journey
- an immersive view of customer lives through diaries, videos and interviews
- a personification of the brand as the hero

A killer stat

Focusing attention on one killer stat from your main data story can sharpen the audience's mind and get them to see the scale of the potential opportunity or threat in a real-world context. It works well when the killer stat is shocking, surprising or thought-provoking – you can then build a story around the statistic, providing context, explanation and implications. By focusing on one killer stat, you reduce the risk of misremembering and misinterpreting the data, ensuring more accurate recall.

However, the downside of using a killer stat for the hook is that it might over-simplify the story, so due consideration is required to ensure it is the right killer stat and it aligns to the overall message and objectives of the data story.

Examples of potential killer stats:

- the monetary value associated with the opportunity or risk to show the size of the prize we can win or lose
- the range between differences in opinion to show diverse and polarizing responses or feelings
- the relative scale of demand or uplift versus a tangible concept such as a visualization comparing the number with the size of a country or the capacity of a stadium
- a quiz to guess the number before the real number is revealed to show difference between perception and reality

Metaphors

A metaphor can simplify a challenging abstract concept and relate it to more familiar and concrete ideas that are already understood, making the data story more accessible to audiences with different knowledge levels. They tap into common knowledge and shared experiences, bridging the gap between what the audience already know and the new data in your story by anchoring any new information in familiar territory. Metaphors are great for creating vivid mental images to help audiences visualize the data for themselves, as well as engaging multiple senses to enhance the storytelling process. However, the downside of using metaphors as hooks is that they are not always understood in the same way across different cultures and languages, making them harder to use with global audiences.

Examples of potential metaphors:

- well-known folk tales and fairy stories with a moral that relates to the customer or brand dilemma
- comparisons to tangible constructs, such as the vast ocean, the high mountain, a bridge, a puzzle piece, etc.

- comparison to other brands in the use of case studies to showcase how others have dealt with similar challenges

Having worked with data storytellers for many years, I have seen lots of different metaphors used to bring data to life. The one that had a lasting impression and I often cite as a great example of the power of metaphor was for a very dry and serious data story to be shared with the board within local government to encourage them to work with external partners to improve how resident data was collected, shared and used to drive real-world interventions. The existing data story was full of graphs and data tables, but when asked to think creatively about the problem in the data story and the impact it was having, they came up with the idea of 'Where's Wally?', who is also known as Waldo, Willy, Walter, Charlie, Holger and Vallu, depending on where you are in the world. In these children's books you must find the character in complex visual images with very few clues to go on – just his hat and glasses. Just like in the metaphor, the data story high-lighted the problems of having lots of contrasting data and very few clues to find the right people and the risk involved with delivering interventions aimed at these hard-to-reach targets. The team were reluctant to use the metaphor for fear of over-simplifying and making a serious data story seem trite, but the director involved loved the idea and purchased a number of the books to use with the board at the start of her board presentation. When she finished, the chief exec-utive stated he wanted all data stories to be as great as that one and asked to borrow the books so he could replicate the same hook when meeting with external stakeholders to address the issue that was now top of his agenda.

Scenarios

Scenarios provide a perspective of a possible future and enable you to explore 'What if?' questions with your audience. They are not predic-tion; they are narratives of alternative outcomes and consequences in which today's decisions may be played out. They may be based on forecasting data or more qualitative scenario planning, but they help bridge the gap between the data story and the practical application of the insights, ideas and recommendations. Scenarios allow for illustration and the painting of a mental or physical picture that provides a tangible output for the audience to relate to. However, scenarios, even if supported by good forecasting data, incorporate uncertainty and variability. They need to be used with audiences who understand the limitations of the data, otherwise they may require so many caveats that they lose their impact.

Examples of potential scenarios:

- a perspective on alternative paths in response to an external trigger or event
- a comparison to an under-performing or failed brand that highlights your fate if the situation gets worse
- painting a picture of the art of the possible your audience can aspire to

A recent scenario hook used by a B2B service brand that proved highly effective involved them taking their internal newsletter format and rewriting the headline summary page with news stories from five years in the future. Each headline story highlighted certain KPIs that had shifted positively and the impact it was having on performance. Having been exposed to this future world the audience had many questions on whether this was possible as an outcome and what they would have to do to get to this end point, thus engaging them with the agenda of the data story and provoking them to generate ideas before the data story even started.

Step 2: Add the personal touch

WHY PERSONALIZATION MATTERS

Personalization in data storytelling enhances engagement by tailoring information to the specific needs and interests of the audience. Customizing narratives with relevant copy, examples and visualizations creates a more compelling and relatable experience. It fosters a deeper connection, ensuring that the data resonates with individuals on a personal level. Personalized data stories are more likely to be

understood and remembered, driving better comprehension and retention of key messages. This approach not only captures attention but
also facilitates more meaningful communication, making the data
more accessible and impactful for diverse audiences with varied levels
of expertise and interest. In the same way that you expect email copy
and insights to be personalized to you as a consumer, tailored B2B
communication is needed to demonstrate your understanding of the
relevant context and to foster trust in your specific recommendations.

> Think about who your audience is and who you are trying to influence.
> Is it somebody who's going to be more numbers and data-driven or is it
> somebody who gets excited by what gives consumers energy when they get
> out of bed in the morning? How can your product fit in with that? You have
> to be flexible in your style, understand who you're trying to influence,
> understand what their needs are, and make sure you're using what you've
> got in the right way so that you really resonate with the people you're
> trying to influence.
>
> **Sinead Jefferies, SVP Customer Expertise, Zappi**

However, if you are to avoid creating multiple versions of a story you
need to think creatively when it comes to personalization. The data
story itself should not be personalized as this has been driven by the
evidence and creating multiple versions will cause confusion, and
possibly chaos! But you can personalize content in a smart way by
how you emphasize different points of view and in the copy you use.

HOW TO PERSONALIZE YOUR STORY
To personalize the data story without creating multiple versions of
the truth you need:

- to pick a perspective
- bespoke, specific outputs

PICK A PERSPECTIVE

> If you're talking to a very customer-centric person you might use a more purist customer angle focused on their pain points, the emotion customers feel and what impact that has in driving them to a competitor. You might lean in on the emotional side, but it is still data based on what customers are doing and saying. But if you're dealing with somebody who's more focused on the commercials then you're still using customer data, but you're using it to tell the commercial story. Here you will focus on how many customers left us, how much that is worth and the impact on market share. In both cases we are going to ask for a budget to do something about it.
>
> **Rhea Fox, Digital Director, Ted Baker**

When it comes to personalization, considering the right angle is imperative. Ask yourself the following questions about the angle you want to take to reach and influence the specific audience:

- Do you want to be controversial?
- Do you have something new to say about the topic?
- What are others saying about the topic?
- How can you differentiate the message by making it more personalized?

> I'm seeing more focus on coming up with either a different or more controversial angle on a topic. If it's a topic that everybody's talking about, take generative AI for example, everybody wants to have something to say, and everyone's pretty much saying the same thing. Can we say something different? Is it going to cut through? Can we back it up with data and research? And if we can, can we own this space? Otherwise, it's not worth us getting involved in the conversation.
>
> **Rachael Kinsella, Editorial and Content Director, iResearch Services**

When picking your perspective, lean on your marketing skills to help you build your audience personas. For example, in the De Beers case study we shared in Chapter 2, the data story was focused on targeting a new segment in the population. But there were two very different audiences to be convinced, with different motivations and needs. This meant that personalization of the data story outputs was required to cut through and engage the different target audiences. Although the De Beers diamond report stayed the same, the story output was personalized to reach and influence the two personas.

> Senior management and the CEO really needed to see what this was going to do to the bottom line. They knew the market inside out, so they needed to understand what the potential was, so obviously we had to make sure we had the right data to show what we expected a performance uplift to be. On the other end of the scale, the jewellers needed to be taken on more of a story about evolving consumers and the world around them, linking this to real people they could really see and feel in their local areas.
>
> **Rosy Harrington, Global Brand Planner, De Beers Group**

BESPOKE, SPECIFIC OUTPUTS

As data storytellers you can leverage the same techniques used in account-based marketing (ABM) when looking to persuade your different internal and external audiences. This means that some of your data storytelling output will have more universal messages, and some will need to be tailored to the unique requirements of specific audience members.

Some ways to personalize your data story outputs include the following:

- Customize the emails that accompany the circulation or distribution of your data story to pinpoint how the data story will help them with their specific needs or pain points.
- Produce specific content to support different stages of the communication journey, such as short educational content for new

starters to the business to quickly inform them of the back story, or 'What's new?' updates for audiences who are already very familiar with the data story outputs.

- Leave a small section in the executive summary to tailor personalized calls to action that you can adapt for different meetings.

- Offer dynamic content as part of the data story outputs to allow audience members to analyse certain elements of the data story in a different way.

One of our expert marketers talked about using data storytelling as part of their ABM strategy to engage external customers with their products and to help position the brand as the expert. Personalization was required for the thought leadership used in their marketing campaigns to speak to the specific needs of decision-makers in each key account. Conversations around different insights were shared between marketing and business development teams to enable those having frontline conversations with decision-makers in the account to personalize the data stories shared in the overall thought leadership. Bespoke content creation led to better customer conversations, which then led to a better understanding of audience needs that could feed into future storytelling and marketing campaigns.

Using data storytelling as a circle of engagement was something I witnessed first-hand when heading up a B2B insight team. A key programme of work involved designing bespoke data stories for a tailored customer experience feedback tool that catered to our top 20 key accounts. The 20 bespoke stories involved rich qualitative data and quantitative benchmarking that we shared with the service directors to enable them to have personalized conversations with their key accounts.

Step 3: Keep the momentum going

WHY MOMENTUM MATTERS

An article written by behavioural scientist Daniel Kahneman and colleagues provided groundbreaking evidence for what is known as the peak–end rule (Kahneman et al, 1993). This study, along with further studies, concluded that people judge an experience largely based on how they felt at its peak (i.e. its most intense point) and at its end, rather than based on the total sum or average of every moment of the experience. The effect occurs regardless of whether the experience is pleasant or unpleasant.

The peak–end rule applies to any interaction or experience where there is a distinctive beginning, middle and end, including a data story. When applying this psychological rule to data storytelling it assumes that people will judge a story based on how they felt at its peak and at the end, rather than based on the total sum of the average of every moment of the story experience. Other information included in the data story aside from the peak and the end is not lost, but it is not used to evaluate how the story made them think and feel. While there is some contention regarding the long-term impact of the peak–end rule and whether the peak or end is more prevalent in recall, the theory does suggest that not all elements of your data story are equal, and some require more care and attention. When applied effectively, the peak–end rule can help make your data story more engaging, memorable and influential.

HOW TO KEEP THE MOMENTUM GOING

To ensure you create a data story that not only captures initial attention but also keeps the momentum through the detail you need to:

- craft your points of view into story peaks
- finish on a high point

CRAFT YOUR POINTS OF VIEW INTO STORY PEAKS

In Chapter 7 we discussed the importance of identifying three to five insight points of view as part of your analysis, synthesis and interpretation of the data. These encapsulate the most impactful insights and recommendations from the data and represent the peak moments in your story. To translate these points of view into peak moments we need to leverage the memory bias for more intensely emotional events. While this does not mean manipulating the emotions of the audience, it does mean highlighting and dramatizing the emotional elements of the story.

To ensure that each peak stands out and makes the necessary impact, there are a number of storytelling techniques you can apply:

- Build a sense of tension leading up to the peak moment by creating a sense of anticipation. This could involve reasserting the complication in your story that needs to be resolved before sharing the point of view and how it will make a difference.

- Identify what emotions you need the data story to evoke. Is this about building empathy for the customer among the audience? Is it to inject a sense of urgency and determination into agreeing an action? Is it about generating a buzz and excitement about the art of the possible? Is it about feeling shame for not adequately addressing a customer pain point?

- Incorporate details that emotionally resonate with the audience. This could include personalizing the point of view to highlight what it means for specific audience members, or linking to a personal first-person story shared in the hook.

- Consider how you will visualize and reinforce the peak moment and engage the senses. This could involve using photographic imagery, infographics, or video or audio verbatim to bring the peak to life visually and through sound.

- Use repetition of key words or images to reiterate the significance of these peak moments and how they connect to the overall narrative.

- Use emotional and descriptive language to describe the peak and bring the human experience to the forefront, rather than business jargon.

FINISH ON A HIGH POINT
Given that the ending is critical for recall, we need to be more strategic about how we finish off our data story.

ENDINGS TO AVOID FOR YOUR DATA STORY

- **Finishing with the most important message**: Saving the most important message to last, thinking it will mean your story ends on a high, is naive. Given poor attention spans and the risk of cherry-picking messages throughout, waiting to reveal the best bit last is high-risk. Chances are the audience switched off after 10 minutes, so your supposed 'ta-dah' ending will be lost. Saving the best for last is about the storyteller's ego and is not audience-centric.

- **Finishing with the same points already made**: While some repetition is useful for aiding processing and recall, too much repetition is a bad thing. Repeating the summary you started with is just plain lazy and doesn't add any further value to the story.

- **Finishing with the last observation in your dataset**: Worse than a repeat of the summary is no deliberate ending at all. Finishing with the data is the easiest way to make the energy levels of the audience fall off a cliff.

- **Finishing with 'Any questions?'** The least memorable way to end your data story is with the question 'Do you have any questions?' By this point any audience questions should have already been addressed – either in advance of communicating the data story or as the data story has been delivered.

- **Finishing with a rational benefit**: Concentrating on the rational benefits linked to your story does not leave the audience with a strong personal outcome. What the audience really want to know is what is in it for them personally to take ownership of the data story and take the recommended decisions or actions. Will this make their lives more fulfilling? Will it help with their visibility and recognition? Will it help build their credibility in a particular area? These are the human motivations that encourage people to act, not arbitrary metrics and targets.

There are different styles that you can choose from when crafting a deliberate data story ending:

Open-ended

For exploratory and highly complex stories, you may not be able to offer the audience a complete and neat ending. An open-ended story might be necessary when only part of the complication can be resolved by your data. The key to a good open ending is to ensure you either resolve some of the issues – with some quick or obvious wins – or give a sense of hope that the work in progress will ultimately provide a more complete answer. The ambition for the ending in this scenario is to ensure the audience care enough to keep the data story alive.

Techniques you can try when an open ending makes sense include the following:

- Personalize the ending to key individuals in the audience by highlighting what they can contribute to the next stage of the story.
- Inspire them to keep the momentum going by painting a picture of what could be possible.
- End with a thought-provoking question regarding what next to encourage further reflection.
- Reiterate why this is still an important data story by reinforcing why it matters.

Co-created ending

Humans prefer their thoughts and ideas to be endorsed and supported by others rather than being told what to do. Often, when there are multiple egos in the audience, giving them a role to play in co-creating the ending, before providing your own version, can be a useful technique to ensure buy-in or for the audience to take ownership of the story direction. The ambition for the ending in this scenario is to ensure the audience are invested enough to play a role in what happens next.

Here are some techniques you can try when a co-created ending makes sense:

- Incorporate a 'choose your own adventure' element to your data story by providing different options or routes that the audience can select and preview potential outcomes.
- Use frameworks that encourage your audience to take the data story to the next level by facilitating divergent thinking and the prioritization of ideas.

- Ask the audience to use the data story to inform the development of a journey map and pinpoint the areas of most importance and where they can influence.
- Ask the audience to create an empathy map to translate the data story into a working plan to meet the needs of the target audience.
- Use a 'How might we…?' question to help the audience build on the ideas from the data story.

Definitive ending

A definitive ending works when we are clearly able to show how the resolution in our data story will help meet the goals and overcome the challenges. In this situation we have permission to think through the practical implications and next steps to achieve these results in the real world. The ambition for the ending in this scenario is to motivate the audience to act.

Techniques you can try when a definitive ending makes sense include:

- making a specific call to action or ask of the audience
- showcasing progress already being made and how the new learnings will help improve this further
- highlighting any successes that have been made by others in the same situation

Putting into practice

A key framework to assist you with creating your data story

Creating a storyboard before developing specific outputs offers several advantages in the process of crafting an effective and impactful data-driven narrative. Storyboarding enables you to visualize the flow and how the various narrative elements we have discussed will connect and progress. By storyboarding first, you can think creatively about what the essential components of the data story are, and what

FIGURE 8.1   The storyboard template

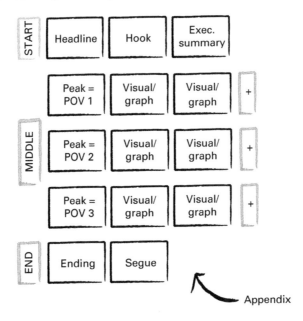

are just 'nice to have' elements that make it too complex or convoluted. By reviewing and editing your storyboard before creating the content itself, you can spot where moments of impact or emotional resonance need to be dialled up or whether the pacing needs to change to keep the momentum going. Storyboarding is also an effective and efficient way of developing your data story and will inevitably save reworking content later in the development of your data story. It is also a good visual tool for sharing, gathering feedback and collaborating on the final story.

Figure 8.1 is a visual representation of a storyboard that ensures a strong beginning, middle and end to your data story. A great storyboard should incorporate the following:

1 The high-impact beginning contains three core elements:

   a. a compelling headline title to encourage the audience to want to find out more

   b. a hook that makes an emotional connection with the audience and primes them to receive the detailed messages

   c. an executive summary which contains the full high-level story from set-up, through conflict, to resolution, supported by the key points of view you want them to recall

2 The strong middle contains three core elements:

   a. an easy-to-navigate structure that follows the argument outlined in the summary and segmented by the points of view

   b. points of view that translate into peak moments in the data story for the audience

   c. only the most relevant data to support the story, with simple visualizations, such as graphs and diagrams

3 The high-impact ending contains two core elements:

   a. a purposeful and deliberate ending that is relevant to your story

   b. a well-managed segue into reflections, conversation, debate or action planning

---

If you want to change the way that you tell a story, you need to do the work upfront and you need to think differently. You need to invest in engaging a wide range of people to build your story and socialize it in the business. That can take more time, and if you're short on resources or have regular deadlines that can be a barrier to doing things properly or differently. Getting buy-in from people can be challenging but it's extremely worthwhile.

Charlotte Neal, Head of Marketing, Turning Point

Challenge 1

Take an existing data story output that you are familiar with and audit for best practice:

- Did the output have a balance between the logical argument, the use of data and the emotional connection or did one dominate more than the others?

- Did the start include a hook to make the emotional connection between the data and the audience?
- Could you clearly identify the three to five story peaks?
- In hindsight, what else might you have considered if you wanted to make the story stronger?
- Given your evaluation, what would you do differently to improve the data story?

Challenge 2

For your revised data story that you have defined and developed in previous chapters, use the principles and techniques covered in this chapter to finalize your storyboard.

Remember to:

- Think creatively about how to hook your audience with a simple but engaging mechanic.
- Personalize your executive summary with a specific audience in mind.
- Ensure the storyboard follows the structure recommended to balance the beginning, middle and end.
- Perfect the tension within your points of view to create peak moments that will draw your audience further into, or back to, your story.
- Challenge your use of evidence and ruthlessly edit to ensure that only what is necessary is included.
- Identify a suitable ending that leaves your audience thinking and wanting more.

KEY TAKE-OUTS

1 Enriching your story with human experience and real-world examples will instantly make it relatable.

2 Look for clever ways to personalize the story without creating multiple versions of the truth.

3 Remember the science behind hooks and the peak–end rule when developing your data storyboard.

Coming up next...

In the next chapter we look at executing a remarkable data story by using our communication and presentation skills to land the message. It will provide ideas to help you design your story outputs, curate a range of digestible micro-content to improve reach, and incorporate interactive techniques into the story delivery to facilitate audience thinking.

References

Dahlstrom, M F (2021) The narrative truth about scientific misinformation, *Proceedings of the National Academy of Sciences of the United States of America*, 118 (15), e1914085117, doi.org/10.1073/pnas.1914085117 (archived at https://perma.cc/R3ZY-VD9X)

Gallo, C (2018) You have 9 minutes and 59 seconds to hook your audience. Here's how to do it in 3 steps, Inc., 31 May, www.inc.com/carmine-gallo/you-have-9-minutes-59-seconds-to-hook-your-audience-heres-how-to-do-it-in-3-steps.html (archived at https://perma.cc/4YLQ-R95B)

Hooper, I (2020) Ten ways cognitive biases impact data design work, Medium, 20 May, medium.com/nightingale/ten-ways-cognitive-biases-impact-data-design-work-be83f86d4274 (archived at https://perma.cc/8E5Y-BWXK)

Kahneman, D, Fredrickson, B, Schreiber, C and Redelmeier, D (1993) When more pain is preferred to less: Adding a better end, *Psychological Science*, 4 (6), 401–5

Zak, P J (2014) Why your brain loves good storytelling, *Harvard Business Review*, 28 October, hbr.org/2014/10/why-your-brain-loves-good-storytelling (archived at https://perma.cc/6HFW-3QB5)

9

How to execute a remarkable data story

In this chapter we will explore:

- the power of a remarkable data story
- the pitfalls to avoid when executing your data story
- the three steps to best practice
  - optimize existing data story outputs
  - curate a range of digestible micro-content
  - incorporate interactive techniques into the story delivery
- putting into practice

The power of a remarkable data story

QUICK RECAP

A remarkable data story requires you to use your communication skills to execute and deliver story outputs that will stand out, disrupt thinking and drive further interest in the topic.

Making a difference

The following case study demonstrates the value of a remarkable data story.

CASE STUDY

Context

A global client in the automotive sector had invested significantly in understanding the customer experience across the purchase and service journeys. Through extensive research and customer data analytics they had a clear picture of:

- the role of each touchpoint on overall brand perceptions and the customer lifetime value metric
- drivers of satisfaction at each touchpoint
- the role of customer communications at each touchpoint

In addition to the data collection and analysis resources, the business had also invested heavily in some great reporting tools to communicate the data to relevant stakeholders, including senior decision-makers and frontline sales and service teams.

Challenge

Despite producing high-value actionable data stories, very few people were accessing or using the tools to incorporate these stories as part of their decision-making processes or their business-as-usual practices. This meant that although the business had the knowledge to improve perceptions, optimize communications, drive purchase consideration and maximize long-term customer value, they were not able to surface and communicate this in a way that had an impact on the decisions, actions and behaviours of stakeholders.

Action

The customer experience team set off on a two-year journey to disrupt the communication of the data stories within the business. We decided to focus on changes that would result in the greatest impact at the lowest cost that would not intervene with business-as-usual reporting on key customer metrics.

Year 1, priority 1: Improve the monthly board report
The existing board report comprised many data tables, graphs and bullet points all squeezed onto an impossible-to-read one-pager. This had been amalgamated over many months based on specific asks from the senior decision-makers to include certain measures but had led to a document that was impenetrable. The accompanying appendix was equally cluttered, with no room for any insightful commentary to draw out the important ideas and recommendations. Even the

FIGURE 9.1 The T-shaped data story communications plan

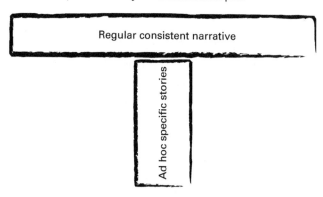

executive summary was a dense, text-filled page and, although it held interesting findings, there was no real story, recommendations or actions.

DEVELOPING A T-SHAPED COMMUNICATIONS PLAN

Figure 9.1 illustrates a T-shaped data story communications plan. The T-shaped plan incorporates the need for both ongoing consistent narratives – the horizontal part of the T shape – alongside ad hoc, time-specific or trigger-specific stories that will stand alone as a narrative while connecting to the bigger picture – the vertical part of the T shape,

- The first step in developing the T-shaped plan was to develop the core story themes for the monthly customer update with a focus on the ongoing brand performance story. This would be based not on the measures that were requested out of interest but determined by the evidence and the key drivers of brand loyalty.

- The second step involved brainstorming ad hoc data story ideas centred on specific triggers, such as a new product launch, a new campaign or seasonal promotions.

- The final step focused on agreeing the appropriate format, channels and media we wanted to incorporate into the plan. For the new board report the summary was designed to both encapsulate the metrics that matter and also provide specific recommendations on actions. It was supplemented by additional pages for the specific trigger story for that month.

To execute delivery of this new report, we set up a new way of working to ensure a more efficient process for insight generation, more timely story development that would incorporate sponsor feedback and more visually appealing data story outputs.

Year 1, priority 2: Create micro-content to share bite-sized data stories with frontline staff

It was clear that the frontline sales and customer services teams who were the end users of the data did not have the time, inclination, data literacy skills or motivation to utilize existing dashboards. So any new content would need to overcome these limitations if we were to land the most important insights to help the teams improve customer communications.

Our solution was to develop a template for the team to create a monthly video summary which would highlight the three most important messages for the month, as well as a training video to explain why the measures mattered. The monthly video summary involved a piece to camera from the team and a do-it-yourself screen cast using PowerPoint and audio voiceover. The video was created in-house to ensure a quick turnaround was achieved in delivery and only a small budget was needed to purchase licences to help with editing the video.

Result

Both year one changes had a significant impact on the level of engagement with the data among the two key target audiences. Not only did the frontline teams start accessing the new assets and using them as talking points in their regular team meetings, the micro-content videos helped drive their overall interest in understanding the customer, leading to an increase in the use of the dashboards.

Outcome and learning

After year one, the new board reporting and video summaries had reached a level of maturity and traction that enabled us to focus on further optimization of the tools and look at what else could improve the communication of the data stories. The optimizations would allow for the team to reset the momentum around the key outputs and drive further reach and engagement across the business. The objectives for year two became:

- showcasing flagship insight stories in customer roadshows
- ensuring a level of consistency across all insight stories
- pushing the gold standard data outputs further into teams

Year two actions

The year two actions were:

- building a relationship with internal communications colleagues to schedule data story campaigns and to utilize existing channels for wider distribution
- building capacity for prioritizing the data story generation and communication alongside business-as-usual
- generating a number of 'best-in-class stories' to tap into the competitive mindset of the sales audience
- creating a digital feedback loop via a comments function in the tool
- refining the video template to incorporate more dynamic content

This case study is a great example of applying communication planning to data storytelling in practice. The dual focus on optimizing what already existed to meet business-as-usual demands and integrating new data story outputs shows that one story output will very rarely do all the jobs you need it to do. The use of the T-shaped plan demonstrates that the value of consistent messaging to reinforce the meta story can be supplemented by ad hoc 'in-the-moment' data stories to provide both breadth and depth.

The pitfalls to avoid when executing your data story

There are three main pitfalls to avoid when executing your data story:

- failing to prioritize time to plan the delivery
- broadcasting the data story at the expense of socializing the message
- ignoring security risks for the sake of creativity

Failing to prioritize time to plan the delivery

It is common to run out of steam towards the end of a project or initiative and there is a danger you might have very little time or energy left to think about how you are going to deliver the data story. Leaving it too late to plan can mean you do not prepare properly.

This can have a negative impact on landing the message, anticipating any challenges, addressing questions or doubts and building consensus on next steps with the audience. According to Jeremy Connell-Waite in his article 'The 72 rules of commercial storytelling' (2019), 'Spontaneous talks are seldom memorable. The best talks involve a huge amount of preparation. Many TED talks have been built upon the 1:10 principle. They spend on average 10 hours crafting their talk for every minute that they present.'

A former boss of mine suggested that for every hour-long meeting I had with a senior decision-maker she would expect me to spend double that time on my preparation and that was on top of creating the data story and the content I planned to share. I have carried this advice throughout my career as it reinforced the fact that creating slides alone was not adequate preparation for influencing outcomes.

Broadcasting the data story at the expense of socializing the message

The reality is that activation of ideas is like a relay race, not an individual sprint. If you spend too much time focused on running your own race and neglect the handover process itself, opportunities to influence the end outcome may be lost. As such, we need to remain laser focused on how the data story will be socialized to ensure audiences take ownership of what comes next.

If you are too focused on merely broadcasting your data story you limit the opportunity to check for understanding, stimulate the conversation and debate, and agree what happens next. Actions to mitigate this risk could include:

- making sure an agenda has been agreed
- circulating suitable pre-reading or pre-watch material
- holding necessary pre-meetings
- ensuring audiences are primed to participate and contribute to the discussion
- making sure potential questions or areas for challenge are surfaced and responses considered
- preparing activities designed to stimulate debate

I remember once a great team member was presenting to a senior decision-maker and I said, 'Are you ready for the meeting?' and she said, 'Oh, yeah, I think I've nearly finished the presentation.' Now that doesn't mean that you're ready for the meeting. She had crafted a beautiful deck, but not thought about what's the point of this and what she wanted to get out of the meeting.

Ruth Spencer, independent data leadership consultant

Ignoring security risks for the sake of creativity

There is a range of great do-it-yourself content tools available that you can access to create infographics, digital brochures, videos, animations, GIFs and so on. However, when using web-based alternative media platforms, you should consider data privacy and security concerns. Be cautious about sharing sensitive business information on external platforms and always check with the experts before signing up and using free licences. Find out what tools already exist in the business that you can utilize to create your micro-content or speak with partners regarding outsourcing.

The three steps to best practice

1 Optimize existing data story outputs.
2 Curate a range of digestible micro-content.
3 Incorporate interactive techniques into the story delivery.

In this section we will look at each in turn, why it matters and how to implement it in practice.

Step 1: Optimize existing data story outputs
WHY EXISTING DATA STORY OUTPUTS STILL MATTER

> I recommend a review of your current data reporting to assess what is adding value. So, refreshing, reviewing and reflecting on the way that you report, manage and act on data within your team. Because if you've got somebody who's having to spend six hours a month on a report that no one reads, there's no point. Then it is about working with people who can guide you through the process of improving what you do.
>
> **Charlotte Neal, Head of Marketing, Turning Point**

We all learn in different ways. Rather than defaulting to what we know or like ourselves, we need to consider what is going to work for others. The VARK model (Fleming and Mills, 1992) identified the different sensory modalities that are used for learning: visual, auditory, read/write and kinaesthetic. We may draw on all four different modes at times, and the creators of the model highlight that 55–60 per cent of respondents studied had multiple preferences. It is worth considering what is your own dominant style and how it might differ from your audience. Review the summary of the four modes below and reflect on how you and your audience like to learn.

VISUAL LEARNERS

In his *Harvard Business Review* article, 'The value of a good visual: Immediacy' (2013), Bill Franks says, 'Our brains are meant to see in pictures. Grids and columns of data, while ubiquitous, make it very difficult to see trends or patterns.' Those who are dominant visual learners like to see ideas and concepts drawn out to make sense of data. They naturally gravitate towards maps, graphs, infographics and diagrams to help understand information. Presentations meet the needs of visual learners if they incorporate images, graphs and diagrams. As those with this dominant mode will be drawn to your slides, rather than any auditory voiceover, it is important that the key messages in your story are highlighted in the visuals themselves, not just explained verbally.

Auditory learners

Those who are dominant auditory learners like to talk things through, and they learn best by hearing ideas and concepts from other people. They favour deep discussions, debates and even arguments, rather than content. Presentations meet the needs of auditory learners when they include voiceover, opportunity for questions and wider discussions. Auditory learners may find visuals a distraction from the oral narrative, especially if they're not completely aligned. They may not be motivated to read documents or pre-reads unless someone is there to talk it through with them. The quality of the narration is important to meet the needs of auditory learners – it requires the right balance of pace, tone and sentiment to get the message across in a compelling way.

> If I look at a big spreadsheet and I have to really try and sift out stuff, I find that really frustrating and boring. But if I sit down with someone and they can talk to me a bit about what's been going on and where this data comes from that helps my understanding of the data and also the context.
> **Charlotte Neal, Head of Marketing, Turning Point**

Read/write learners

Those who are dominant read/write learners are a fan of the written word and like lists, hierarchy and structure to their content. They draw meaning from the words used in headings, titles and commentary and appreciate clarity and brevity. Read/write learners are happy to work with written rather than presented documents, if they are well structured and easy to follow. For time-poor read/write learners, the key message needs to be spelt out clearly in a few bullets in an email, while presentations meet the needs of read/write learners through the use of executive summaries and the commentary used on the individual slides. In meetings and presentations, they are just as likely to write their own notes or doodles to help explain the content, rather than rely solely on the content itself. Hard copies of the slides or physical assets they can access will be appreciated.

> I think platforms like Canva are going to be critical. The majority of the data outputs in our industry are probably written on PowerPoint and Keynote, but I think everyone is frustrated as they are too constrictive and it's just not creative enough for great storytelling. I think platforms like Canva are bringing an element of creative, playful storytelling and fun to what was traditionally quite a dry business presentation.
>
> **Jake Steadman, Global Head of Market Research and Data, Canva**

Kinaesthetic learners

Those who are dominant kinaesthetic learners require ideas and concepts to be demonstrated rather than explained. They value application, real-world examples and case studies. As they learn through problem solving and interaction, rather than being told the key messages, they may benefit from reviewing the data themselves in the spreadsheet or data platform in advance of a formal presentation of results. Getting their hands dirty with the data manipulation, rather than relying on the interpretation of the data provided by others, helps them to understand the data story. This can be the hardest segment to reach via traditional presentation formats, but incorporating real-world examples, case studies and interactive exercises such as quizzes and polls, alongside the standard deck of slides, can go a long way to meet their needs.

Presentations have become ubiquitous as a communication tool to deliver learnings, because, when done well, they can be helpful for all four modes of learning. While many have predicted the demise of the PowerPoint presentation over the last couple of decades, the reality is that it is still the medium of choice for the majority of businesses.

HOW TO OPTIMIZE EXISTING STORY OUTPUTS

To maximize the value of existing outputs in traditional formats, you need to:

- rethink your data visualization
- create powerful commentary

RETHINK YOUR DATA VISUALIZATION

Given visuals play a significant role in data storytelling, they are a great functional tool to help our audiences interpret the evidence we are prioritizing to tell our data story.

> When it comes to supporting visuals, they need to pop with the message – you shouldn't have to explain it. And people shouldn't have to work hard to read it. It should just pop and smack them in the face with the facts or story you want to tell – it should be punchy, powerful, but ultimately easy to read – no matter how complicated to derive in the first place.
>
> **Lizzie Harris, Customer Director, B&Q**

When optimizing your visuals, you need to assess which is the most suitable graph type to get across the message you are trying to convey. Richard Wurman (2000), architect, graphic designer, author and creator of the TED conference, argues that although information is infinite, the ways of structuring it are not. He identified five different methods to structure information using his LATCH acronym as a useful tool to consider the right graph for the job:

- **Location:** Information can be organized by its physical location, such as on a map or in a directory. When the key message is focused on space, place or location the following options work well:

  - Maps are the most intuitive way to show location data and the rise in geographic information system (GIS) software has enabled users to create ever more creative data maps, such as heat maps showing different usage patterns over geographic areas.

  - Scatter plots represent data points in a two-dimensional space and are useful when looking at the relationship between different brand attributes relative to a defined axis.

  - Flow maps illustrate the movement of objects or people between locations. These are helpful when visualizing traffic flow in a retail space.

- **Alphabet:** Text-based information that needs sorting to make it more coherent can be presented alphabetically. This technique can be useful when looking at sentiment and text analysis from unstructured data sources. When showing information organized alphabetically the following options work well:

  ○ Word clouds visually represent the frequency of terms or names by varying the size of the text based on their occurrence and can be a good visual way to summarize large datasets of unstructured information, such as text analysis generated from social media scraping.

  ○ Tables are a useful means of presenting alphabetical data when you need to show detailed information, such as lists of names, titles or text-based records.

- **Time:** Information can be organized by time, such as trends, milestones, stages, journeys and processes. When your story requires a key focus on progression or change over time the following options work well:

  ○ Line charts display data points over a continuous time or numeric scale, with lines connecting the data points, and are often used for tracking trends and changes.

  ○ Area charts are like line charts but fill the space below the line, making them suitable for showing cumulative data trends and where you want to highlight the total trend, as well as the individual sub-elements.

  ○ Flowcharts illustrate processes or workflows, showing the sequence of steps, decisions and actions within a system over time.

  ○ Gantt charts are project management diagrams that show tasks or activities on a timeline and are useful for tracking progress.

- **Category:** Information can be organized by category, such as by topic, type or function. When showing information organized categorically the following options work well:

  ○ Venn diagrams and matrix charts depict the relationships between sets or categories, showing the commonalities and differences between them. They are useful for organizing information and making comparisons.

- Bar charts are used to represent data with discrete categories. They show data as horizontal or vertical bars of varying lengths, making it easy to compare values. Stacked bars are effective for illustrating the composition of a category to show how each category contributes to the whole.

- Pie charts display data as a circular graph divided into slices, where each slice represents a proportion or percentage of a whole. They are effective for showing parts of a whole, but use them wisely – the brain struggles with reading angles and so works best with two or three categories to compare, rather than many categories.

- **Hierarchy:** Information can be organized in a hierarchical structure using a predefined set of criteria, such as 'most to least important'. When showing information organized hierarchically the following options work well:

  - Mind maps are hierarchical diagrams that help visualize relationships between a central idea and related subtopics.

  - Tree diagrams represent hierarchical structures, branching out from a central node to show relationships and subcategories.

  - Indented lists such as bullet points work well for simple hierarchical text-based data.

Deciding on what type of visual best suits the key message you want to get across will stop you from defaulting to what you already have in your templates and tools.

Further enhancements of the visual element of your existing data story outputs can be made by utilizing standard design principles. Below are some basic principles, but if in doubt consult with an expert, experiment with different ideas in data visualization tools, or look online for inspiration.

DESIGN PRINCIPLES

- Stick to one primary message per visual. This keeps your data story clear and prevents overwhelming the audience with complex graphs.

- Use relevant visual cues like annotations or callouts to emphasize the most critical information within your data visualization – but don't overdo it (see next bullet!).

- Keep your visualizations simple and uncluttered by removing any unnecessary elements or distractions that don't contribute to the understanding of the data.

- Embrace white space to create a clean and uncluttered look, making your content more accessible.

- Edit and refine multiple times to eliminate any unnecessary elements. Every element should have a purpose.

The mindset that we need to adopt when optimizing the visuals in presentations is simplicity and that less is more. This is not about dumbing down and over-simplifying but making it as clear as possible so the eye can focus on the most important information.

CREATE POWERFUL COMMENTARY

Words have power. The words you use to communicate the points of view can make the difference between the audience finding your data story merely interesting and informative versus being motivated to take action. In crafting your points of view, you can use the 4Us principles (urgency, usefulness, uniqueness, ultra-simple) as a checklist for effective copywriting. The 4Us were created by author and entrepreneur Michael Masterson as part of his work with the American Writers and Artists Institute and the Accelerated Program for Seven-Figure Copywriting and is a near-universal tool for writing effective copy:

- **Urgency:** Convey why the insight is time-sensitive or why it's crucial to act now rather than later, or explain the potential consequence of delaying action.

- ○ The use of deadlines, milestones or tipping point in your points of view can demonstrate urgency.

- ○ The use of verbs can also be helpful as they are doing words and can be urgency-triggering for audiences.

- ○ Urgency can help gain immediate attention and action.

- **Usefulness:** Your point of view should demonstrate how it helps in answering the killer question and resolving the conflict, as well as linking to the tangible benefits of acting on your recommendations.

  - ○ It should focus on the practical utility of the information you will be using to support your point of view and articulate the practical applications.

  - ○ Making claims relating to potential impact and outcomes that tie to commercial benefits and use the language of business will get your audience's attention.

  - ○ Usefulness particularly helps when you are looking to demonstrate that you understand the audience and why this data story matters to them.

- **Uniqueness:** The audience don't want to hear the same generic stories so find new perspectives or nuances related to this specific story.

  - ○ Showcase unique data sources or methodologies that were used, and highlight distinctive findings or insights that are not widely known.

  - ○ Personalizing the story for different audiences will make the data story feel unique even if the message is consistent.

  - ○ Uniqueness helps when you are looking to build rapport with the audience.

- **Ultra-simple:** Your point of view needs to be succinct, without any unnecessary embellishment, vagueness or over-generalization.

  - ○ Using universal language that is easily understood, rather than overly complex, theoretical language or jargon, will help keep it simple and concrete.

  - ○ Use precise numbers to illustrate your points of view or reference case studies or real-life examples that are known and understood.

  - ○ Ultra-simplicity helps when building credibility and expertise.

For example, we might inject the 4Us into our example points of view by making the following changes to the copy.

From:

> There are unmet needs we can focus on, such as the high chance of winning, transparency and interesting bonus prizes, *but* the market is already saturated, *therefore* we need all messaging to reinforce these benefits as part of a distinctive positioning.

To:

> There are unmet needs we need to be the *first to own* [urgency], such as *the high chance of winning, transparency and interesting bonus prizes* [useful], but the market is already saturated with *little opportunity to bring in new users versus switching* [ultra-specific], therefore we need all messaging to reinforce these benefits as part of a distinctive positioning *by focusing on X, Y and Z* [unique].

From:

> HCPs have significant time constraints that limit device demonstrations or trainings, *therefore* resulting in habitual prescribing based on experience, *but* without overcoming this significant barrier we will have limited opportunity to gain product adoption.

To:

> HCPs have *only two hours a month available* [urgency] for device demonstrations or trainings, therefore resulting in habitual prescribing based on experience, *which leads to the dominance of competitor A* [usefulness], but without overcoming this significant barrier by providing *alternative ways to access the information* [unique], we will have limited opportunity to hit our *product adoption target of X* [ultra-specific].

Step 2: Curate a range of digestible micro-content

WHY MICRO-CONTENT MATTERS

In addition to your optimized data story outputs, you need to utilize other communication tools to help your data story reach a range of audiences, often outside a meeting format. Developing micro-content to tell your data story can offer three key advantages.

Advantage 1: Preventing information overload

In a world of constant distractions, it's crucial to cut through the noise and convey your message quickly. Micro-content is more likely to capture and retain the audience's attention than a long and complex presentation and it forces the storyteller to distil complex stories into their most essential components. Incorporating micro-content into your communication plan allows you to design with a distracted audience in mind and focus on short, easily digestible and engaging outputs.

Advantage 2: Increasing flexibility and usage

Micro-content is designed for sharing and can increase your reach and engagement with a broader audience, while at the same time tailoring messages to specific audiences with content that is highly relevant to their needs. You are unlikely to tailor different versions of a presentation deck due to complexity and time constraints, but micro-content is quicker and easier to personalize for the specific audience. Micro-content is ideal for A/B testing and experimentation to understand what resonates best with your audience, while getting large-scale feedback on a presentation deck is unwieldy and slow.

Advantage 3: Increasing the ease of consumption

Micro-content is easier to consume and understand on the go. It's more accessible to a wider audience, including those with limited time or those who want to consume content on small screens. As micro-content lends itself to more visual tools it can also be repurposed across various platforms and media in a way that a presentation deck finds hard to do.

HOW TO INCORPORATE MICRO-CONTENT INTO YOUR DATA STORYTELLING

To ensure you make the most of the communication opportunities available you need to:

- think digital and physical
- tap into existing channels

THINK DIGITAL AND PHYSICAL

> We developed a communications campaign to help the global insights
> team. They are all doing research studies focusing on their area in lots of
> different countries around the world, but what they needed was a curated,
> editorial view of it all. They've got data over here, got data over there.
> They've got trends. They've got Mintel reports. So, we pull that together,
> curate it as an editorial exercise and create much more consumable content
> like a *New York Times*-style article, videos, infographics, blogs – three or four
> things a month. Many are short films, a lot of them are observing trends on
> social media. Then we share them with the wider organization internally –
> and that has had an amazing impact. It's basically been a really good source
> of inspiration for innovation and R&D. It's not just the insights sitting in a
> PowerPoint report. It's getting them to think, 'What are we going to do
> about this?' I feel like it's created a really visceral understanding of the
> customer.
> **Lucy Davison, Founder and CEO, Keen as Mustard Marketing**

There are many different digital tools to help generate micro-content.
The most popular include:

- infographics
- video
- screen casting
- interactive quizzes
- GIFs and memes
- blogs and newsletter articles
- podcasts
- white papers
- ebooks

The choice of digital micro-content depends on your data story, your
target audience and the platforms you have available for distribution.

But don't forget the role that non-digital content can play. By allowing for a more tactile and multisensory experience, non-digital micro-content can stand out and make a more personal connection with the audience. To this day, the most utilized and in-demand insight communication I created was a series of short, printed and bound A5 compendiums of each key competitor. As part of running the marketing analytics team I was also responsible for competitor intelligence and the compendiums were designed as a pre-read for a workshop where we were going to play war games to stress-test a particular marketing strategy. Each compendium provided a detailed data story on a key competitor we would be using in the war game. Each workshop attendee was supposed to just have one booklet each in preparation for the competitor they would be playing in the game. But all the attendees asked to have access to all the booklets, not just for the workshop itself but for future reference. Even stakeholders not involved in the workshop were demanding copies for themselves, so we had to organize multiple extra print runs. By making it a useful data story and an exclusive tangible asset, we ended up creating in-demand data content.

In addition to flyers, brochures or booklets, consider other forms of physical content, such as swag, posters or meeting room decorations. In-person micro-content might include a short speech in a 'town hall'-style forum or a practical demonstration. These can be video-recorded for digital repurposing and edited into even smaller bite-sized content.

When I was at Twitter we talked about the theatre of research, which is partly about how we told stories, and partly about the medium we used to tell that story. We tried to put on a show. We did things like invite hundreds of people to a venue and do live neuroscience. Very few graphs, very little data, make it heavy on the 'lols'. It was putting on a show, but ultimately delivering the key insight that we needed to deliver. It wasn't always in person, though. Sometimes it was an animation, or a video or a physical bit of swag. The common thread between all those stories was this idea that we had to put on a show and there was theatre to that if we were to convince people and be memorable.

Jake Steadman, Global Head of Market Research and Data, Canva

TAP INTO EXISTING CHANNELS

Tapping into existing communications channels offers several advantages that can enhance the reach, impact and effectiveness of your data story. These channels might include your own intranet site, existing newsletters, knowledge-sharing platforms or digital tools like internal social media platforms. These channels already have established audiences so you can reach people without having to build something new from scratch and are already a trusted source of information.

Utilizing tools that can track your audience can help you to learn about behaviours and preferences to adapt your future content and stories. I would also actively encourage participation with the content by turning on features such as likes, comments and shares, to gain input and feedback on your data story. See these channels as another means to answer questions, provoke thinking and engage in conversations around the topic.

> I also think there's something about the semi-permanent distributed nature of work now that is having an impact on how I tell stories. Post-Covid, some people are back in the office all the time, but most of us are working some kind of hybrid now, and I don't see that changing. That means you have to find different ways of telling stories. I think the distributed nature of work and the platforms that we use to communicate in that distributed environment are going to force a change in how we tell our stories.
> **Jake Steadman, Global Head of Market Research and Data, Canva**

Step 3: Incorporate interactive techniques into the story delivery

WHY INTERACTION MATTERS

Despite all the communication tools we have at our disposal to reach busy people, when it comes to influencing decisions and actions, it can be hugely beneficial to meet with others, at the same time, ideally in the same place, if feasible. Pushing for a meeting, face-to-face or virtual, has three key advantages.

Advantage 1: Socializing plans, ideas and insights to build consensus

Sharing output in a meeting environment can socialize insight and build consensus around the recommendations regarding decisions and actions. Being in the same meeting ensures that those with differing views can be exposed to the same data story and work towards agreement and alignment on the best course of action. Feeling part of the process and being given a chance to have a say is more likely to lead to an increase in commitment and support from others.

Advantage 2: Generating input to refine the final story message

For data stories that are works in progress, sharing early storylines in meetings can facilitate input from others than can help shape the final story. With the right audience in the meeting, you can present your data story and gain feedback and constructive criticism to help refine how the story is positioned. Bringing in members from cross-functional teams at this stage can both highlight and help integrate diverse perspectives on the data story and assess what that means for the decision.

Advantage 3: Encouraging buy-in and accountability of the actions

For data stories that require immediate action, reinforcing the argument and making the ask in a meeting with the relevant decision-makers and action takers can sharpen minds, drive urgency or make a burning platform feel more real. With the right people in the meeting, decisions can be collectively made and the process fast-tracked to the next stage. Even with data stories where buy-in of the recommendations has yet to be achieved, holding a meeting as a mid-point discussion to air challenges and issues can help. These meetings can focus on agreeing on the next steps even if there is no consensus on the end goal.

HOW TO INCORPORATE INTERACTION WITH THE DATA STORY

To ensure the meeting is more than sharing the data story outputs, you need to:

- leave space in your agenda
- spark a conversation

FIGURE 9.2 The ideal meeting structure

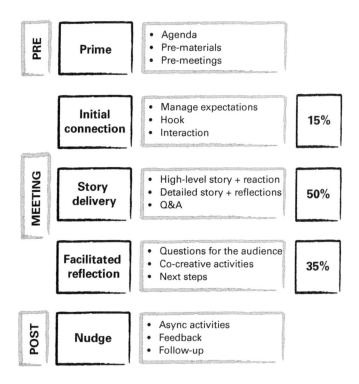

LEAVE SPACE IN YOUR AGENDA

My own golden rule for data storytelling is only use 50 per cent of the time you have with your stakeholder audience to share the data story. As Figure 9.2 shows, this 50 per cent should be the middle part of the meeting and include landing the key messages, covering the necessary detail required to support your messages and dealing with specific questions about your data story. The other 50 per cent of your time with the stakeholder audience should top and tail your story delivery.

As shown in Figure 9.2, we have allocated 15 per cent of time for the beginning of the meeting, where you will make an initial connection with the audience, and 35 per cent for the end of the meeting, where you will facilitate a conversation.

In reality, if you have a 30-minute time slot to make your case, you have only 15 minutes to share the story and are unlikely to be able to present more than two or three slides. If you have an hour scheduled this would mean no more than 30 minutes presenting content – so probably a deck of 12–15 slides. Bear in mind that most individuals cannot concentrate beyond 20 minutes anyway and this is why TED talks are limited to 18 minutes (Connell-Waite, 2019). Guy Kawasaki's (2005) 10/20/30 rule of PowerPoint also supports this level of restraint, suggesting a PowerPoint presentation should have 10 slides, last no more than 20 minutes, and contain no font smaller than 30 points.

This concise approach has implications on how you use your time effectively that we address in the following tips:

- **Tip 1:** Think creatively about how you use the time outside the meeting itself. If you have only limited time in a meeting or on a call to get your data story across then you are going to need to think about utilizing simple pre-reading or pre-watching micro-content in advance. This will encourage buy-in from the audience by building confidence in your ability to make the most of the time available and can get the audience up to a certain knowledge level or level the playing field. You might also need to prioritize pre-meetings with key sponsors or audience members who can provide valuable feedback on how to distil your message for the audience and who can help you land the message in the meeting itself. You might also need to consider any supplementary content you need to prepare if some of the audience expect to access a more comprehensive view of the data story in their own time.

- **Tip 2:** Focus on the initial connection. At the start of the meeting:
  - reiterate the expected outcome you are looking to reach by the end of the meeting
  - share the agenda and how the meeting is going to run to ensure you get to the outcome
  - outline your expectations of them and their role in the process
  - get them engaged and motivated on the topic

This could be as simple as reasserting an agenda, followed by sharing your story hook, or as complex as conducting a short ice-breaker activity following up on any pre-reads or activities. The key at this point is to ensure they are focused on the present – not their 'to do list' from their last meeting or when they are going to get lunch. By grounding in the present and giving them the direction of travel, you automatically instil a level of confidence into your audience. You are demonstrating that you know what needs to be done and are in control. This makes the audience feel that you can be trusted to optimize the time available and will offer a suitable value exchange for their participation.

This initial connection becomes even more powerful when working virtual and informal communication is minimal. Resist the urge to jump straight into the data story.

o **Tip 3:** Deliver the data story with impact. When it comes to presenting your data story, remember that your audience may have a short attention span. This means starting with the short version of the data story in the executive summary. Telling the high-level story in the early part of the presentation not only shows confidence in what you are recommending, but also provides the opportunity to take a strategic pause to check initial responses to the message and tailor the detailed content delivery to the areas that require more understanding or persuasion.

Chunking the content down using the principles shared in this book and using deliberate strategic pauses to encourage reflection and questions throughout will make the presentation feel more interactive. Inject reflection points at key stages in your presentation and use verbal cues to manage expectations around feedback, questions or challenges.

SPARK A CONVERSATION

Connell-Waite (2019) cited a keynote he attended given by Gary Vaynerchuk, the entrepreneur, speaker and author, when, 'in the 1-hour keynote he spoke for only 12 minutes and then conducted a 48-minute Q&A with audience, creating a masterclass in audience engagement'.

Here are a number of ideas to help you spark a meaningful conversation about the data story:

- **Ask for initial reflections.** If short on time, or when handling a big audience, you might not be able to have a detailed discussion but that doesn't mean you cannot capture initial reflections on the data story. If the meeting is in person, you can capture quick reflections on Post-It notes, or if meeting virtually via chat function or whiteboard tools. This could then kick-start a follow-up conversation from that feedback.

- **Give the audience a task.** Give your audience an active listening task before diving into the details – this way, they are consciously listening throughout, rather than playing a passive role. Active listening tasks also provide ready-made conversation starters. This could be as simple as asking them to listen out for the two or three points that are most relevant to them, or as complex as giving them a role and asking to listen to the story through the lens of a customer segment or competitor.

- **Ask the audience to 'think back'.** One of my favourite ways to get the audience involved and to spark a productive conversation is to deploy a 'think back' exercise towards the end of the presentation. For example, I might say, 'Before my final slide containing next steps/thought starters/calls to action, I am going to pause and ask you to co-create that page first in pairs based on what you have heard in the story.' These are then shared among the wider group to ensure different perspectives are heard. It also allows the data storyteller to reinforce ideas, actions or plans, rather than prescribe them – leading to greater accountability among the audience.

- **Offer a mechanism for further questions.** If you don't have much time to answer questions as you go along or at the end of the meeting, you could prepare some FAQs of your own to share. Or you may request any additional questions are posted in the chat so you can answer offline afterwards as part of the follow-up.

- **Ask a brilliant question.** Finishing a presentation by asking 'Any questions?' is a surefire way to kill the experience. You are better off asking an interesting, challenging or provocative question of the audience to ensure they create a positive end experience in their own mind.

QUESTIONS TO STIMULATE DEBATE AROUND YOUR DATA STORY

To check understanding of the data story:

- What has been a real aha!/surprise/what has sparked interest?
- What is the best/worst thing that could happen now?
- What's the one thing you want to change (based on what you just heard)?
- What are the implications and risk?
- What does this mean for us/our brand/product/plans?

To explore options highlighted in your data story:

- What are you already doing/planning to do that addresses these issues/ opportunities and what else are you now thinking?
- What scenarios can we foresee?
- When have we been successful in a similar situation in the past and what can we learn from that experience that applies here?
- What's getting in the way of our progress?
- If this was your own business, what would you do?

To help develop accountability of decisions and actions off the back of the data story:

- What is within your control to do something about?
- What will you do differently in the next couple of weeks/immediately?
- What are the next steps towards achieving the end goal?
- What are the options moving forward? Now? Next? Never?
- What if competitor X acted on this first?

Putting into practice

Challenge 1

Reflect on a data story you have recently shared and review against best practice:

- Did you utilize a campaign approach and consider the use of micro-content to support the main presentation delivery?

- Did the presentation of the content itself take less than 50 per cent of the time with the audience?

- Did you have lots of clarifying questions about the data in the charts?

- Did you have time to instigate a facilitated conversation to gauge reaction, check for understanding and provoke some early responses?

- In hindsight, what else might you have considered if you wanted to make the execution of the story more effective?

- Given your evaluation, what would you do differently to improve the delivery of the data story next time?

Challenge 2

For the revised data story that you have defined and developed in the previous chapters, use the principles and techniques covered in this chapter to develop your communications plan.

Remember to:

- Use the T-shaped plan shared in the case study to think about what approach works for each type of story.

- Think beyond a PowerPoint presentation and incorporate micro-content into your approach.

- Ensure the agenda for any meeting follows the golden time rules and leave enough time to make an initial connection, answer questions and facilitate a conversation.

- Prepare where your strategic pauses might need to come during your delivery and the questions you want to ask of your audience.

- Identify the success criteria for your delivery that you are looking to achieve that can easily be measured to evaluate progress.

KEY TAKE-OUTS

1 Don't forget that significant improvements in communicating your data story can be achieved by optimizing traditional outputs like PowerPoint.

2 See the communication of the data story as a campaign, rather than a one-off piece of content, and consider what additional methods, media and channels might help you to maximize reach and impact.

3 Don't use up all your time, energy and head space creating the data story content itself. Remember, you need time and effort for the delivery as well.

Coming up next...

In Part Three we move away from the specific skills and tasks involved in the data storytelling roadmap and look at the wider mindset, ways of working and processes that enable you to embed the skills in practice. We will focus on becoming a data storytelling champion and how to develop a data storytelling team culture.

References

Connell-Waite, J (2019) The 72 rules of commercial storytelling, LinkedIn, 22 October, www.linkedin.com/pulse/72-rules-commercial-storytelling-jeremy-waite (archived at https://perma.cc/3RGZ-TMG6)

Fleming, N D and Mills, C (1992) Not another inventory, rather a catalyst for reflection, *To Improve the Academy*, 11 (1), 137–55

Franks, B (2013) The value of a good visual: Immediacy, *Harvard Business Review*, 21 March, hbr.org/2013/03/the-value-of-a-good-visual-imm (archived at https://perma.cc/6EA6-ZVCZ)

Kawasaki, G (2005) The 10/20/30 rule of PowerPoint, Guy Kawasaki, 30 December, guykawasaki.com/the_102030_rule (archived at https://perma.cc/D9XP-RYNG)

Wurman, R (2000) *Information Anxiety: What designers need to know about the information age*, Mayfield Publishing Company, California City

PART THREE

Becoming a data storytelling champion

10

The mindset and ways of working for a data storytelling champion

In this chapter we will explore:

- how to make data storytelling stick
- what makes a data storytelling champion
- the mindset and ways of working to build a data storytelling culture

There's a misperception that all marketers have to have the numbers and the qualitative perspective and do everything. Recognize what your strengths are. Find a way to be an influencer, while still being true to yourself. Be really focused on being the best you, not just being some kind of carbon copy of an excellent data-driven marketer.

Sinead Jefferies, SVP Customer Expertise, Zappi

How to make data storytelling stick

In Part Two we focused on the data storytelling roadmap, providing a step-by-step guide to developing a great data story. In Part Three we look at moving beyond the steps, skills and capabilities involved in developing great data stories to focus on what it means to become a champion responsible for building a wider culture of data storytelling within the marketing function.

The biggest reward as a trainer and coach is going back into teams six months, a year and two years after delivering development programmes and seeing the practices and behaviours taught embedded in the team. I love hearing feedback from those who have taken the learnings and made a conscious decision to apply them in practice, to experiment with what works for them and to persist with a change in behaviour, even when busy or under pressure. It is even more rewarding when they share the feedback they have received from their end audiences about the impact the data story has had on their ability to make or support decisions and take action.

The impact of quick incremental wins

In a recent storytelling showcase session, we reviewed progress since the formal training workshops. As we celebrated success and shared story examples, I was struck by how even small storytelling changes had made a significant impact on how individuals approached their work and the immediate feedback they were receiving from their stakeholders.

When sharing what had worked, they called out the following:

- Focusing on the killer question not only gave them structure for their content, but it also shaped their approach to information gathering up front and where they focused their energy at the interpretation stage.

- By holding themselves to account as to whether each element of the story content had a clear 'So what?' or 'Now what?', they were able to be more ruthless in their storytelling and more concise in their outputs.

- By focusing on compelling titles, clear headlines, insightful commentary and simple visuals they had more high-value conversations with end stakeholders and greater levels of engagement.

The examples they shared were varied, including:

- The creation of a one-page visual summary that demonstrated the key components of successful income-generating campaigns. Stakeholders have now asked for this data story to be expanded to a wider dataset and replicated for other types of campaigns.

- The use of two killer questions to provide strategic-level evaluation of all partnership marketing activity. Evaluation outputs are now providing different activation teams, in both the organization and the partner companies, with an understanding of the bigger picture impact and the role of the different activities and campaigns in driving overall success.

- A simple data visualization supported by relevant real-life examples of marketing activities was used to bust a myth on the role the brand plays in a key social issue. This data story has been used to support negotiations with a potential new partner to invest more in the issue.

What makes the difference

Over many years supporting teams with their data storytelling skills, I have sought feedback on what changes have been implemented and what practices, activities and behaviours made the biggest difference. There are a number of consistent factors shared by teams that have truly embedded a data storytelling culture.

1 **Keeping data storytelling on the agenda.** This means it is seen as an ongoing topic of discussion, knowledge shared and skills development. They don't just tick the box by upskilling individuals and assuming 'job done' – they look for more ways to keep the momentum going.

2 **Holding each other to account.** Through collaboration and giving constructive feedback they ensure continuous improvement. They are not afraid to seek input and ideas from others in the endeavour of getting to a better and more actionable data story.

3 **Translating the learnings.** After applying the techniques in practice, they create their own principles for data storytelling, coupled with suitable templates, checklists, guidelines and case studies.

4 **Empowering passionate individuals within the team.** They create dedicated storytelling champions who proactively support others to develop and embed the skills in practice, as well as finding new ways to stretch their own skills in this area.

What makes a data storytelling champion?

To be a data storytelling champion you do not need to be the best data storyteller. As highlighted in the McKinsey behaviour archetype matrix (Kirchherr et al, 2023), a champion is already putting in a high level of practice in a chosen area and has a high desire to keep improving. Being the best at something doesn't make you a champion – being prepared to persevere and learn from mistakes is key. Being able to take others with you on the journey, to provide support and encouragement to those who are also looking to develop their skills, and to design and embed structures that will enable practices to become a normal way of working is more important than being the best data storyteller.

The champion role requires the data storyteller not only to get involved within their own team and support others in their function, but also to advocate externally for data storytelling. This relies on building strong, trusted relationships outside of the marketing function to influence others without the formal authority of being their manager or having a say in what they do and how they do it.

To perform as a champion:

- Be motivated and passionate about the benefits that data storytelling has to offer.
- Advocate for the time, resources and budget needed to improve data storytelling.
- Build alliances with the right people to create and promote great data stories.
- Engage in training to build expertise and look for best practice that you can learn from.
- Role model the data storytelling behaviours and ways of working to others.
- Coach and inspire others to raise awareness of the role and benefit of data storytelling.
- Assess and demonstrate the impact of data storytelling investment and initiatives.
- Communicate accomplishments and shout about success.

For example, take our data storytelling champion, Thomas. Working as a media strategist, Thomas is already a highly competent data storyteller, but he knows he could be more consistent in his own practice, could always look for incremental improvements to enhance his data stories and help others that he works with to improve their own data storytelling skills. Thomas is motivated by going beyond the data to uncover the truths driving audience behaviour and has spent time working closely with colleagues across planning and data to build his understanding of existing tools and datasets.

Using well-known industry tools such as TGI and Google Analytics, alongside other primary and secondary sources, Thomas uses his audience insights to shape communication strategies and his data stories to support his creative, design and editorial colleagues.

After attending training, Thomas volunteered to be put forward for the champion's programme. His manager was pleased as she felt he would be perfect for the role, but wanted him to want it for himself, so he would be motivated to make the most of the opportunity. Working with the sponsor for the programme and with input from his fellow data storytelling champions, Thomas put into place an activation plan which was pitched to the director of the agency and incorporated a range of ideas to support data storytelling, including leveraging existing tools even harder, designing new checklists, crib sheets and a 'story finder' tool to assist the wider team, and adding new scoping, analysis and retrospective sessions to the project workflow.

ARE YOU READY TO BECOME A DATA STORYTELLING CHAMPION?

Are you:

- passionate about data storytelling and the benefits it can bring to the marketing function?

- keen to stay up to date on new data storytelling tools and techniques?

- motivated by coaching and mentoring others in their data storytelling journey?

The mindset and ways of working to build a data storytelling culture

There are five key mindsets to enable great data storytelling:

1 Begin with the end in mind.

2 Stay curious.

3 Think story continuously.

4 Embrace the mess.

5 Collaborate with purpose.

Mindset #1 – Begin with the end in mind

Ask yourself, who are we trying to reach? What story are we trying to tell? What hypothesis are we trying to test? Not thinking about that at the outset and then trying to reverse engineer it – that doesn't work. You need to be aligned at the starting point.

Rachael Kinsella, Editorial and Content Director, iResearch Services

WHAT DO WE MEAN BY 'BEGIN WITH THE END IN MIND'?

In his book *The 7 Habits of Highly Effective People* (2004), Stephen Covey shares in his second habit, 'Begin with the end in mind', the need to define clear measures of success and plan how to achieve them. This habit is about your ability to use your imagination and to envision the end goal. Unless you make a conscious effort to visualize the outcome you are trying to achieve, then you empower other people and circumstances to shape the outcome by default.

KEY BEHAVIOURS AND WAYS OF WORKING TO SUPPORT THIS MINDSET IN PRACTICE

Beginning with the end in mind encourages intentional planning, leading to more meaningful and effective outcomes. As a data storytelling champion, you can demonstrate and role model this mindset:

- **Keep in touch with events in the wider business.** It is so easy to get stuck in our silos, but bringing in a broader understanding of the business (commercially and operationally) can ensure your data story is based on what is feasible and actionable.

- **Review your archives.** Look back into your archives and evaluate which data stories made a significant impact. Keep track of the different data stories and the key topics of interest to highlight consistent patterns that can feed into future data storytelling plans. Valuable questions to ask to assess the impact of previous data stories include:

  - How many people did the data story reach?
  - How many people opened and shared the outputs?
  - How many people contacted the marketing team with follow-up questions?
  - What was the audience feedback on the data story?
  - How has the data story been used for decision-making?

- **Create your own frameworks.** Similar stories can be repurposed for similar topics and business questions. These are your story archetypes and can offer a go-to structure and storyboard to refine for future data stories. While each data story will have its own unique evidence and recommendations, the structure of the argument and points of view may be relatively consistent within an archetype. Using predetermined structures that are tried and tested saves reinventing the wheel.

Mindset #2 – Stay curious

Stay curious and constantly look beyond the usual or the expected.
If you're working in FMCG, or whatever sector, don't just look at what your competitors are doing there. Don't just stay within that lane. Get out of

your lane. See what's happening elsewhere. Read different reports or listen to podcasts or ideas to get a different perspective to your own. One of the things we used to do all the time would be consciously breaking the rules. So, for example, if you're trying to get sales to cross-sell a new SKU, or upsell, look at who does that well – not just in your sector. Investigate how they do what they do – what's their model? Who can we talk to in that industry about that? What can we learn from that?

Rosy Harrington, Global Brand Planner, De Beers Group

WHAT DO WE MEAN BY 'STAY CURIOUS'?

A mindset that stays curious will incorporate a strong desire to learn, explore and understand the world. Despite the well-known benefits of curiosity to business performance and culture, research by Francesca Gino at Harvard Business School (2018) shows that leaders are often resistant when it comes to encouraging curiosity for fear of making individuals harder to manage and the perceived trade-off between curiosity and efficiency. Therefore, finding ways to stay curious when under time pressure to deliver and facing short-term goals can be difficult and will require intentional practice. It is unlikely that you will be able to invest excessive amounts of time making new discoveries in the datasets, but there are a number of ways you can inject curiosity in short bursts to disrupt any default thinking and to keep an open mind. By staying curious, data storytelling champions will spot the meta stories that cut across individual plans, strategies or projects. These are the data stories that deserve to be heard but aren't always being called for.

KEY BEHAVIOURS AND WAYS OF WORKING TO SUPPORT THIS MINDSET IN PRACTICE

Curiosity encourages time and head space for asking questions, which can lead to new insights. As a data storytelling champion, you can demonstrate and role model this mindset:

- **Spend more time immersed in the world of your customer or target consumer.** Observe qualitative research or get out in the field and do your own intercept interviews with customers in situ. Ask agencies or insight partners to organize accompanied shops or visits with different customer types.

- **Keep abreast of best practice.** Read widely about marketing, consumer psychology, retail trends and the macro environment in which your customers operate. Having a broad view of the bigger picture can ensure you bring a range of ideas to your data storytelling. Gain inspiration by expanding your network and attending events, and generally get out of the marketing bubble.

- **Try new ideas.** Conduct experiments, test hypotheses and make early inferences and predictions before committing to further exploration. This could be A/B testing in a live environment to test two different versions of digital marketing, or multi-variant testing in labs to test different combinations of copy, images and headlines.

- **Take note of where the critical knowledge gaps are.** Consider what questions are harder to answer and create a plan to address the gap. This might mean advocating for access to sources not budgeted for or investment in the right tools for the job to enable you to make the most of the data already available.

Mindset #3 – Think story continuously

One of the key things we found when we worked with Coca Cola EMEA was that stakeholders were interested in the data or insight when it was 'their' project, but they were not interested in it when it wasn't their project, because they'd moved on. Not only that, but the rest of the organization, beyond the core stakeholders, had no knowledge or understanding of what the consumer insights team were doing. And this is the world's leading consumer brand. Insights were not actually cascading out throughout the organization. The role of the marketing person is to stop being so project-focused and think much more broadly about the organization and the future.

Lucy Davison, Founder and CEO, Keen as Mustard Marketing

WHAT DO WE MEAN BY 'THINK STORY CONTINUOUSLY'?

If you view data storytelling as a back-end task aligned to a specific project, you risk not having the time, energy or inclination to build good practice into your work. Tight turnarounds on projects and deliverables can mean there is no extra capacity to build in these additional storytelling tasks to your processes. Another risk to seeing data storytelling as a back-end task aligned to a specific project is that you can miss the opportunity to ensure that any new ideas and insights uncovered that do not relate directly to the project are lost in the vacuum.

While some data stories will be tactical and serve a specific purpose for a predefined project, many data stories will run and run – just like a 10-season blockbuster drama. These stories may require greater reach and complex buy-in and are unlikely to be completely resolved. For example, consumer needs and expectations are constantly evolving based on their experiences in the wider world, so it is unlikely you will ever have a perfect solution for their needs that lasts forever. Instead, you will constantly be looking to understand how those needs are evolving and what it means for your brand, products and services. Just when one conflict appears to have been overcome, the next one is around the corner.

These are the meta stories that need to be top of mind throughout, regardless of some of the day-to-day data stories required for business-as-usual performance measurement. By thinking of data storytelling as a continuous activity, you give yourself permission to share early insights, discuss findings with others, seek additional data and incubate ideas without committing to a set deadline for sharing a specific data output. This allows data stories to emerge and develop more proactively and organically and data story content to focus on the work in progress and the evolving narrative, rather than an arbitrary end point.

KEY BEHAVIOURS AND WAYS OF WORKING TO SUPPORT THIS MINDSET IN PRACTICE

Thinking story continuously encourages incubation and iteration, which can lead to the identification of early data stories to watch out for and more comprehensive data stories that can evolve over time.

As a data storytelling champion, you can demonstrate and role model this mindset:

- **Integrate data stories into key marketing documents.** Keep the customer front of mind by integrating the meta story into your marketing strategy and communication plans. By putting the customer at the heart of your marketing thinking it will help you avoid the trap of distractions, tangents and 'nice to have' activities.

- **Create feedback mechanisms.** Incorporate learnings from customers, end audiences and stakeholders into your evolving meta stories. Developing small virtual groups or communities of interest focused on the meta story and involving key stakeholders and partners can provide valuable input and feedback on the story over time.

- **Look out for early warning signs.** Look out for any changes in the regular data feeds, as these could be early warning signs of potential issues or new opportunities. Not every update requires an iteration of the data story output, but they can be shared informally to gauge reactions, stress-test relevance and evaluate how they might be incorporated into future content. These updates and feedback may in turn throw up more ideas for further investigation.

- **Celebrate progress in data storytelling.** Recognize quick wins or small achievements in moving the narrative forward. Taking stock and calling out progress are especially important in ongoing high-level data storytelling, as they focus the mind on what transformations in awareness, understanding and influence have occurred to date, and can motivate and inspire further effort and interest.

Talk regularly about insights. Make sure that you're finding a story or a surprising insight or something to have a five-minute conversation about on a regular basis. It doesn't even have to be from within your organization. It can be a stat that's come from an external source that you might want to have a conversation about. Just make sure it becomes part of your ongoing conversations with your team. Try and make it part of the narrative, so it feels really natural. That will improve your familiarity and engagement with data, but in a less formal way.

Charlotte Neal, Head of Marketing, Turning Point

Mindset #4 – Embrace the mess

> When we think about data, about data science, about analytics, it is very quantitative, performance-focused. Brands tend to focus on measuring what they do. There is some amazing analytics work being done but it's very focused on measuring your ripples through an ecosystem. And that's great, but there's another whole world out there. It's the messier side of data, which doesn't lend itself very nicely to these data science techniques. But that doesn't mean it's not useful and typically it's falling between the gaps. The gap is a sweet spot where lots of powerful forces are at play that are being completely missed. My point is that if you don't understand the entire world of the data, you're going to miss it. There is blind faith in analytics, which is important, but it's missing these other elements. You need insight into why and where people enter a category, and then what are the stages in that process? You need to make sense of the world aligned to the way consumers see it.
>
> **Jeremy Hollow, Founder and CEO, Listen + Learn Research**

WHAT DO WE MEAN BY 'EMBRACE THE MESS'?

Harford (2020) argues that messiness is essential for creativity and resilience. He also stresses the importance of accepting that data is imperfect, and insight is rarely linear. Rather than sticking to the safety of what you know, including overly simple heuristics and generic marketing rules, great data stories are generated from more nuanced analysis and circular interpretation. This means data storytelling champions need to get comfortable with iteration, uncertainty and knowledge gaps. You need to be prepared to go around in circles a little before the answers to your questions reveal themselves. You need to be prepared to be wrong about hypotheses and actively seek to disprove existing thinking to generate insights worth telling stories about. This also means not just relying on reports generated from the data by experts or other teams but getting closer to the data itself and observing for yourselves. This hands-on approach to data analysis and building your own understanding of what story the data is telling you means less reliance on generic reporting. To break away from your natural instincts to take the prescribed easy route and force yourselves to sit with the uncomfortable mess takes practice.

KEY BEHAVIOURS AND WAYS OF WORKING TO SUPPORT THIS MINDSET
IN PRACTICE

Embracing messiness encourages immersion, sense-making and critical thinking skills, which can lead to a greater understanding of the nuances in consumer behaviour, motivation and perceptions. As a data storytelling champion, you can demonstrate and role model this mindset:

- **Get more familiar with key datasets, definitions and assumptions.** Play with the filters on dashboards and reporting tools yourself or ask the data product owners or your insight colleagues to sit down with you and give you a demonstration of a new tool.

- **Investigate the data from a different angle.** Consider breaking down samples by interesting behaviours, not just standard demographics, or looking at some of the outliers and what they tell us about preference.

- **Conduct interim analysis.** Review data at regular intervals, not just after all the data has been curated and visualized. Getting your hands dirty with the data early on gives you more time for deeper exploration around interesting insights to gain a more nuanced view. It also enables early detection of any data quality issues, facilitating any necessary workarounds or expectation management that might be required.

- **Provide safe spaces for others to experiment with the data.** Find ways to make others – whether your teammates, peers, data experts or partners – feel comfortable with being uncomfortable, embracing divergent points of view, managing contradictory data and challenging interpretations.

- **Bring in expert support to brainstorm ways to fill knowledge gaps.** Those with research and planning skills can help with any additional consumer insights, while data analysts can help with managing any experiments, and data scientists can help with any predictive modelling to help generate proxy measures where data gaps exist.

- **Hold or participate in data story hackathons.** Working sessions can be a great catalyst for creativity and innovation. Designed around real-world customer challenges or business questions and focused on exploring data and creating data narratives within a constrained period, they can yield great results in a relatively short amount of time.

Mindset #5 – Collaborate with purpose

At Aviva we had a customer segmentation, which was all tagged on the database, but didn't really live and breathe. So, we brought it together with the brand strategy to decide on the execution and what we were going to action for each group as part of a customer strategy. What worked for us was having a multidisciplinary working group from across the spectrum. All the disciplines involved were meeting regularly and sharing insights. The CEO liked it because he could see how it can be used.

Rhea Fox, Digital Director, Ted Baker

WHAT DO WE MEAN BY 'COLLABORATE WITH PURPOSE'?

Making sense of your insights to ensure that they are correct, clear, concise and compelling is unlikely to happen looking at a screen. It requires an immersive approach, with collaboration and input from others. *Doing* tasks like reading reports or creating presentations often requires us to be productive, while *thinking* tasks such as insight generation and data storytelling require us to let the mind wander, percolate and bounce ideas around. Purposeful collaboration is not the same as getting feedback on your data story. It requires clear goals, roles and responsibilities and effective tools to facilitate the exchange of insights and ideas. Purposeful collaboration ultimately needs to offer a win–win to all of those expected to contribute. Poor collaboration can be a huge time and resource drain – and a massive demotivator. Purposeful collaboration is a deliberate and structured approach to working together effectively.

Purposeful collaboration encourages both creativity and organization, which can lead to more actionable and valuable insights. As a data storytelling champion, you can demonstrate and role model this mindset:

- **Break down the silos.** This doesn't mean demanding a restructure; means being actively involved in sharing and being interested in what others are doing. Talk about the insights from your data stories and encourage others to ask questions or add their perspective.

- **Leverage your network from across the business.** Bring in diversity of thinking early in the data storytelling process. If you haven't got a great network, build one. Then actively encourage divergent opinions to challenge blind spots and ensure that a range of perspectives feed into your early story hypotheses and data interpretation. You may even encourage people to take on specific roles to avoid 'group-think'.

- **Think laterally about collaboration.** Often when we are limited timewise, we tend to collaborate with those we work with and who are familiar with our work. Gaining outsider perspectives is hugely valuable so consider whether it is appropriate to bring in agency partners, subject experts or academics. Can you even partner with other brands?

- **Develop a community of interest.** Connect with like-minded individuals, data professionals and potential collaborators to focus on the development of a specific data story. This network can be used to explore the insights, draft the outline narrative structure, and create the storyboard framework. Collaborative working sessions with the group can also be used to develop prototypes or drafts of the data story content.

At Sainsbury's we used 'the power of two' relationships, where we paired up analytical people with marketing managers. We implemented 'the power of two' structure throughout the team, so at a senior leadership level there was power of two and then all the way down to your communications executives and your analysts on the ground. They would then go off and influence and educate in the business in pairs, bringing together both views, and jointly telling the story of marketing performance. That was our way of getting credibility and building trust.

Lizzie Harris, Customer Director, B&Q

When you think about the end-to-end lifecycle of inspiring a customer to take action, in getting them onto our website, exploring and understanding our products, ultimately purchasing, and then building a relationship with us, that's a very holistic way of looking at a customer. To make that a reality requires a series of different skill sets and both data and marketing are key parts of it. They need to work together to a single plan that has the full customer lifecycle in mind. I think it is very important that you're part of a cross-functional squad, working towards a clear goal. What doesn't work is when marketing has to come up with a plan and the data team are delivering models that don't line up to the plan. And then what you end up with is a whole bunch of brilliant models that go nowhere and a whole bunch of amazing marketing that could have been optimized, and we know after the fact because it's not really doing very well. I also think it's worth bringing the research team in as well as data because there's so much that we don't know about our customers because their world is beyond our company.

Sanica Menezes, Head of Customer Analytics, Aviva

KEY TAKE-OUTS

1 Don't just focus on developing your skills and capabilities; think about building a sustainable culture of data-driven business decision-making.

2 Embrace the data storytelling champion role by experimenting with new ideas, seeking inspiration and role modelling the right mindset.

3 Being a data storytelling champion is most effective and rewarding when collaborating with others.

Coming up next...

In the next chapter we look at shortcuts, tools, checklists and guides to help data storytelling champions embed the skills and ways of working in practice.

References

Covey, S R (2004) *The 7 Habits of Highly Effective People: Restoring the character ethic,* revised edn, Free Press, New York

Gino, F (2018) The business case for curiosity, *Harvard Business Review,* hbr.org/2018/09/the-business-case-for-curiosity (archived at https://perma.cc/5UBP-T7X9)

Harford, T (2020) *Messy: How to be creative and resilient in a tidy-minded world,* Riverhead Books, New York

Kirchherr, J, Mayer-Haug, K, Rupietta, K and Störk, K (2023) Archetyping to create lasting behaviour change in organizations, McKinsey, 23 October, www.mckinsey.com/capabilities/people-and-organizational-performance/our-insights/the-organization-blog/archetyping-to-create-lasting-behavior-change-in-organizations (archived at https://perma.cc/3UCD-BFBJ)

11

Streamlining your data storytelling ways of working

In this chapter we will explore:

- how to run an effective data storytelling session
- how to leverage data storytelling shortcuts
- how to continuously improve data storytelling capabilities

We need to all get better at using data, talking about it, collaborating, and then building the story. But we need to be able to do it in a nimble and agile way. It can take a really long time to review data, to spot trends, to create reports, to build out narratives, to socialize them, and it can feel like you are just figuring it out as you go. That can be really hard. So, a shortcut can be a good thing. As a result, we can spend more time thinking about the customer and how to engage them.

Charlotte Neal, Head of Marketing, Turning Point

How to run an effective data storytelling session

As a trainer, coach and facilitator, I have developed an efficient and effective data storytelling planning workshop that has evolved out of thousands of hands-on sessions. This is a two-to-three-hour session and allows for focused discussions and collaborative work to develop robust data stories. I recommend conducting this type of workshop at the interim analysis stage as part of an iterative process, rather than at the end of all the data gathering and analysis or after content has been produced. This ensures the time invested in the workshop will deliver greater efficiency at the later stages. For a data storytelling champion leading and facilitating the workshop it will involve a full day of time to do the necessary preparation and pre-work before the workshop, plus the time taken afterwards to process the outputs of the workshop and to generate the draft storyboard. In addition to the data story planning workshop, you might also consider additional sessions to collaborate on developing the hook, designing new outputs and building a communications plan.

A guide for a data story planning workshop

Having a workshop guide is crucial for aligning team members and staying on track. Below is an example plan for such a session.

Expected outcomes (15 minutes):

- Reiterate the primary goal of the session and what the end outcome looks like – this should have already been shared in advance of the session.

- Provide a clear visual roadmap for how you will get there, including introducing and explaining any frameworks you plan to use to support the process.

Context setting (20 minutes):

- Clarify the target audience for the data story and discuss their specific needs, using a persona template if required.

Data overview (30 minutes):

- Provide background information on the datasets you are using for the work and the key variables and metrics to focus on.

- Summarize any significant macro-level trends observed so far at the interim stage.

- Brainstorm task to agree:

  o What are the key points from the overview that *reinforce* what we already know?

  o What *new perspective or angle* can we bring to this?

  o What *new news* or insights are starting to stand out?

  o What are some of the *conflicts and tensions* the overview has highlighted?

Defining/redefining the killer question (25 minutes):

- Either use an existing killer question agreed at the scoping stage or develop the question in the session itself.

- If refining, check against any new insights and ensure a proper killer question.

- If developing in the session, provide a master list of prompt questions and get the group to sort them into priority groups based on relevance to different audiences and those that are critical vs nice to know.

- Agree consensus on the killer question.

- Using the checklist shared in Chapter 5, sense check the killer question before moving on.

Break (10 minutes)

Sharing key insights (30 minutes):

- Present a high-level view of the synthesized themes at a micro level – you may find using a simple framework can help support this rather than detailed PowerPoints or dashboard outputs.

- Discuss definitions to gain consensus around themes and wordsmith if required.

Converting insights into your story (40 minutes):

- Prioritize key themes in a sorting exercise, and for priority themes brainstorm key implications for the audience.

- Structure at a higher order level, aiming for three or four key groups that will form your points of view.
- Draw out the narrative flow visually based on discussions so far and seek feedback and reactions.
- Incorporate any builds into the narrative flow visual.
- Discuss any areas of contention and what will need to be managed.

Next steps and action items (10 minutes):

- Discuss the next steps in the data story development process and plans for drafting the storyboard.
- Assign responsibilities for reviewing the storyboard before developing the story content.
- Set a timeline for completion and distribution of the draft storyboard.
- After the workshop session, draft a simple storyboard using the template shared later in this chapter, incorporating the inputs and ideas gathered from the workshop. This should be circulated as an output from the session and to stimulate any further feedback or contributions.

To access a digital version of the guide, plus supplementary templates and frameworks to use in a data storytelling planning workshop, go to the supporting webpage for the book at www.datastorytellingin marketing.com.

How to leverage data storytelling shortcuts

Why use story archetypes?

Story archetypes are recurring narrative patterns and themes found in your marketing or communication-related data stories. These archetypes can serve as a guide for story development, helping those creating the story content with a blueprint for constructing engaging and impactful data stories.

There are a number of advantages to generating story archetypes, including:

- providing a clear and structured narrative framework that is already understood
- utilizing familiar narrative structures that are easy to remember and make the message stick
- tapping into universally appealing themes that resonate with the audience
- leveraging tried and tested human experiences that are already proven to evoke a powerful response
- providing consistent structure across different communication platforms to strengthen the messaging
- allowing for flexibility to ensure the data story is adapted for the specific audience, objectives and communication goals
- reducing the time and effort required for story development where agility of messaging is of the essence

While everyone can benefit from data story archetypes, the role of the data storytelling champion is to spot these patterns and themes, to devise the relevant archetype for their function, and to produce template structures to support the repurposing of the story archetype in future storytelling.

Common data story archetypes for marketing and communications

Some typical story archetypes to look out for within a marketing and communications context are set out below.

ARCHETYPE 1: THE PROVEN SUCCESS STORY

This archetype revolves around showcasing positive outcomes and success achieved through marketing efforts. It typically starts with a problem or challenge faced by the company, followed by the strategic implementation of a marketing plan, campaign or initiative. The conflict resolution normally results in the achievement of a key milestone, supported by the data-driven evidence which shows the impact of the marketing effort on business KPIs, such as sales or market share.

In this story archetype the brand is the protagonist, overcoming obstacles and achieving success, while customers play supporting characters who have benefited from the product or service.

ARCHETYPE 2: THE CUSTOMER JOURNEY

This archetype focuses on the customer's experience throughout the purchase decision-making process or the product or service lifecycle. It typically starts with the customer's problem or need, followed by the role of the brand in optimizing the experience over the course of the journey through various touchpoints. The conflict resolution normally results in the customer finding a solution to their problem, supported by the data-driven evidence which shows optimization of the experience. In this story archetype the customer is the protagonist, navigating their way through the marketing funnel, while the brand and marketing channels play supporting characters looking to help the customer on their journey. The role of marketing as the hero in the transformation focuses on the team's commitment to understanding and addressing customer needs and how customer feedback informs marketing strategies.

If you're stuck on how to get started with data storytelling in marketing, always start off with the customer. Put the customer at the heart of your story. Start with what the customer is doing and feeling and experiencing, then think about what you want the customer to go on and do. That's always going to be a really good place to start. That's going to give you a really good spine to hang your story off.

Ruth Spencer, independent data leadership consultant

ARCHETYPE 3: THE SHIFTING SANDS

This archetype focuses on changing trends in needs, expectations and marketing effectiveness over time. It often begins with the identification of a market trend, a change in consumer behaviour, or a shift in competitive landscape. The conflict and tension in the story centre on how the brand will respond, with the conflict resolution addressing the new strategies and tactical adjustments required to either capitalize on emerging opportunities or mitigate potential threats. The trend itself is the character in this archetype, with the brand, customers, competitors and external players acting as supporting characters influencing the response to the trend. The role of marketing as the hero in the transformation focuses on how successful campaigns will improve the brand position, and drive sales and brand growth.

ARCHETYPE 4: THE UNDERDOG

This archetype focuses on key external challenges to the brand – from competitors, regulators or wider macroeconomic or social factors. It often centres on the ongoing struggles and obstacles that impinge on any marketing effort, with the conflict resolution addressing how the brand has been able to achieve success (even incrementally) against the odds. The marketer is the protagonist in this story archetype with the narrative structure highlighting the resilience and determination of the function to overcome challenges through innovation and workarounds.

ARCHETYPE 5: THE DISCOVERY

This archetype focuses on innovation and new opportunities to carve out for the brand. It often centres on the need to tap into unexplored markets, underserved customer segments or unmet consumer needs. The conflict resolution focuses on the role of new and novel marketing approaches to help reach and fill these gaps. The data is the protagonist in this story archetype with the narrative highlighting the key discoveries from the various datasets. The role of marketing as the explorers in the story focuses on the function utilizing these discoveries to implement new ideas and drive positive business outcomes.

These different archetypes help marketers craft compelling narratives that resonate with their audience and facilitate a deeper understanding of the data-driven insights being presented. They draw on repetition of known narrative structures to land the message and aid memorability, as well as offering the data storyteller a good place to start when developing their specific story.

To access our visual guide to finding the right data story archetype, go to the supporting webpage for the book at www.datastorytellinginmarketing.com.

Why use checklists and templates?

Creating effective data stories requires a thoughtful approach to ensure that the narrative is clear, compelling and actionable. But when we are busy or under stress it is easy to default to previous ways of working. As such, checklists and templates can be a useful reminder to guide you through the process. While templates can sometimes be seen as rigid and creatively limiting, managed with a degree of flexibility they enable the data storyteller to create a consistent approach to sharing stories, including a standard approach to structure, headings, fonts and colours, etc. A well-designed template can enhance the clarity of your data story by organizing information in a logical and easily understandable manner.

In this section we share a number of checklists and templates that you can adapt for your own data storytelling practices.

THE DATA STORYTELLING CHECKLIST

When coaching data storytelling champions, I work with them to develop tailored checklists that work for their specific team needs. Below is an example of a typical checklist.

- Have you clearly articulated the purpose of your data story, including the transformation you are looking to inspire?

- Do you understand who your audience are and their level of expertise and interest in the topic?

- Do you have a killer question that works as an anchor for your story and ties the data points together?

- Have you developed a compelling hook that sets the stage for the data story?

- Have you included some background information to ensure your audience understand the context of the data, including the end outcome you are looking to achieve and some of the issues that are faced? This could include any relevant industry trends, market conditions or external factors that may impact the story.

- Does the storyline follow a narrative structure that includes the conflict and resolution?

- Have you included actionable recommendations, implications or next steps in your data story resolution?

- Does your story include three of four key points of view that support your story resolution and synthesize your learnings from the data?

- Have you addressed any counterarguments in your narrative and considered how you will deal with any challenges or questions?

- Have you integrated real-life examples such as case studies or customer stories to make the data story feel relatable and concrete?

- Are the data visualizations you have used clearly aligned to the story and do they make the data more digestible? This means checking labels, annotations, scales, etc.

- Have you tested the data story with a small sample of the target audience to get feedback?

THE EXECUTIVE SUMMARY TEMPLATE

The power of a one-page executive summary lies in its ability to capture the most critical information in a visually appealing and easily digestible format. A bespoke executive summary enables us to distil complex data stories into concise insights for specific decision-makers. This is your short-form version of your content for the audience to read, listen to or watch, and as such it needs to be restricted to one or two pages or five minutes of audio or video commentary.

Best practice for one-page executive summaries includes the following:

- Distil to the most relevant information only – this is where your work on your narrative arc and your key points of view will come into its own.

- Start with the most compelling point first – this is what will capture and hold the attention of the audience.

- Use well-structured formats to make reading the commentary easy for the audience – think like a newspaper and go for portrait for text-dominant summaries.

- Use headings, subheadings and bullet points to break up any detailed text and draw the eye to what matters most.

- Personalize summaries based on different audience needs by highlighting specific calls to action or recommendations.

- Incorporate some visual elements to break up text, such as charts, graphs, diagrams, icons or images.

- Embed hyperlinks to encourage the audience to find out more about the data story if they wish.

Here are some of the critical elements to include any executive summary template structure:

- A paragraph/column framing the situation:
  - objective of the data story and definition of success for the topic
  - key metrics related to the data story and aligned to wider goals
  - current performance against goals, targets, benchmarks, etc.
- A paragraph/column isolating the conflict:
  - highlight any performance issues
  - spell out barriers or constraints impacting on success
  - identify potential risks to progress

- Clearly state the killer question as the anchor to your story
- A paragraph/column highlighting the answer to the question:
  - actionable recommendations including any proposed changes to existing plans or initiatives
  - future outlook – tied to either opportunities to be gained or threats you might face if you do nothing
  - high-level commentary regarding timeline, including any milestones or deadlines
- Three or four bullet points covering the points of view that provide the rationale behind your answer
- A closing statement reinforcing the ask or call to action

You may notice that there is very little data itself in the executive summary, except any relevant key metrics that the audience should be familiar with. This is deliberate. An executive summary is not a list of the key findings in the data; it needs to be a well-constructed short story based on the data interpretation and judgement.

THE HEADLINE REPORT TEMPLATE

This template is for the five-slide version of the story (Figure 11.1). This is a story version you would deliver in a 30-minute webinar or as part of a 45–60-minute meeting with questions and debate.

FIGURE 11.1   Headline report template

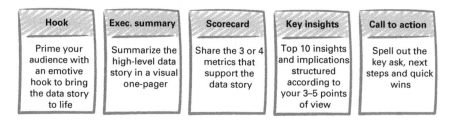

The five-slide template would include the following key slides:

1 The compelling hook to prime your audience.

2 The executive summary that showcases the two-minute version of your story.

3 A high-level performance scorecard with the relevant KPIs highlighting trends and comparisons to any benchmarks.

4 The top insight takeaways from the data that informed your story – five at the most. If more are needed then consider how to prioritize or organize them into higher order themes.

5 The call to action that is relevant for the audience – this could be a key ask, next steps or quick win actions.

This version of the data story has a little more data than the executive summary but is still light touch when it comes to including tables, graphs and key data points. While the high-level scorecard will provide some data to support any trends or comparative analysis, the insights slide will be a visual and text summary of the top takeaways, rather than specific data visualizations.

THE DETAILED STORY TEMPLATE

This template is for the 25–30 page version of the story. I would recommend creating this as a readable document, rather than presenting something this long. You would typically need a two-hour meeting to do justice to presenting and reflecting on a 30-page report. It could be in a digital published format with interactive navigation, but it is unlikely to be a dashboard, as it needs to be narrative-led rather than data-led. This will contain more data than our executive summary and headline report but will not be as exhaustive as an evidence pack used in the appendix or the detailed dashboard that contains all the data points. Within a 30-page report using the template structure below, it is unlikely for data visualizations to account for more than one-third of the data story.

Again, each template should be tailored relative to the story archetype, but I have highlighted below a consistent way of structuring the detailed report. This detailed version of the report would be split into different sections to aid navigation.

Section 1 (4–5 pages):

- Foreword – from a key person of influence sharing an editorial comment on the data story
- Compelling hook – a human story, case study or illustrative example
- The executive summary (as above)
- Definitions – this might include pen portraits of targets or market maps highlighting key territories

Section 2 (around 20 pages):

- POV 1 commentary
  - Key insight 1 – visualization and commentary
  - Key insight 2 – visualization and commentary
  - Key insight 3 – visualization and commentary
  - How any of the key insights vary – by market, customer segment or time period
  - Illustrative example using a case study of good or bad practice
  - Implications and actions – specific recommendations for this POV
- POV 2 commentary
  - Key insight 1 – visualization and commentary
  - Key insight 2 – visualization and commentary
  - Key insight 3 – visualization and commentary
  - How any of the key insights vary – by market, customer segment or time period
  - Illustrative example using a case study of good or bad practice
  - Implications and actions – specific recommendations for this POV

- POV 3 commentary
  - Key insight 1 – visualization and commentary
  - Key insight 2 – visualization and commentary
  - Key insight 3 – visualization and commentary
  - How any of the key insights vary – by market, customer segment or time period
  - Illustrative example using a case study of good or bad practice
  - Implications and actions – specific recommendations for this POV

Section 3 (2–3 pages):

- Summary of learnings and implications
- Call to action
- Provocative statement or question to fuel thinking and debate

There are additional ways to support navigation of a long form read aside from a well-structured story. Below are some example features that can be integrated into your template:

- Incorporate interactive elements like a clickable graph that allow readers to explore the data further if they choose to, rather than forcing them to look at too may dimensions in a static visual. You can also use clickable commentary where a video or audio description goes into more detail.

- Include pop-ups to provide additional context or information when readers hover over specific data points or keywords.

- Add a progress bar or page numbers to help readers understand their position within the data story.

- Periodically include summaries or recaps to reinforce key points and help readers stay oriented, especially in lengthy narratives. The end of each point of view would be a logical place for these.

- If the data story is presented digitally, ensure that it is responsive and accessible across different devices. Consider mobile-friendly layouts for readers on smartphones or tablets.
- Use hyperlinks strategically to provide additional context, definitions or references to related content. Be cautious not to over-use them, as it can be distracting.

THE BESPOKE TEMPLATE

The concept of a bespoke template sounds counterintuitive. But, managed well, it can provide a level of consistency across stakeholder and customer communication, while allowing for tailored recommendations and a degree of personalization that the headline report and detailed reports cannot. By providing support via a template, alongside training and coaching from data storytelling champions or capability teams, it enables other relevant stakeholders, such as sales or category management, to adapt the data story themselves in a way that doesn't contradict the marketing story. It also means that the marketing team are not having to produce multiple versions of the same story. This is true data democratization!

The template guide for a bespoke version of the story enables other stakeholders to adapt the story for the very specific needs of the people they need to influence and ensures all teams are seen as credible experts in the consumer, customer, market or category, regardless of their levels of data literacy.

For example, I was working with an industry body representing a key food sector that was looking to influence retailers to drive category growth. To ensure ownership of key insights across the board we designed a communications plan that leveraged the headline report to drive engagement with the data story and gauge initial reactions to the key insights. Feedback was sought through key partner relationships from the specific buyer audience within key retailers, to ascertain which elements of the story were most relevant to them and their plans. From this, the industry body and their direct clients in the production and manufacturing end of the sector were able to use the template for a bespoke presentation to tailor different versions of the story to share in one-to-one meetings. The template meant that the key messages were consistent but enabled the end data storytellers to provide audience-specific recommendations around product and format mix, as well as key messaging on packaging and in-the-aisle marketing, rather than generic suggestions that didn't meet their specific category plans.

In another example, I was working with a pharmaceutical marketing team who were looking to improve the use of data storytelling in their B2B communications to healthcare providers and generate more personalized thought leadership. We used the bespoke template to ensure a seamless and consistent look and feel between white papers and sales presentations.

To access digital versions of the checklists and templates, go to the supporting webpage for the book at www.datastorytellinginmarketing.com.

How to continuously improve data storytelling capabilities

Measuring success

Improving data storytelling to increase impact requires time, resources and even sometimes budgetary investment. To demonstrate the return on investment we need to be able to show the impact on key measures of success. As data storytelling champions, it is important to identify what success looks like and how you will measure it over time. This requires you to evaluate how effective your data stories are in communicating the insights, engaging the audience and driving decision-making. Below are a number of tried and tested measures to consider for your own evaluation.

Measure of success: Data storytelling leads to greater clarity and understanding of key insights

Metric: Audience comprehension of the main message

Measurement: Audience feedback and reflections shared in meetings

Measure of success: Data storytelling communicates useful insights that align to objectives

Metric: Audience engagement, interest and participation during story delivery

Measurement: Audience asking questions of the data story and relating back to goals

Measure of success: Data storytelling results in greater recall and retention of key messages

Metric: Audience replay key messages and key visuals

Measurement: Degree of recall in follow-up discussions

Measure of success: Data storytelling leads to actionable insights

Metric: Audience utilizing data story for decision-making

Measurement: Tracking changes to strategy or modifications to plans

Measure of success: Data storytelling empowers the audience to share insights

Metric: Audience repurposing and sharing in conversations with their stakeholders

Measurement: Audience feedback and surveys to capture confidence and capability

Measure of success: Data storytelling makes insights more readily accessible to a wider audience

Metric: Audience reach and accessing of data story content

Measurement: Tracking how many people access and distribute the data story

To access our data storytelling audit tool and assessment tools to help with defining your own measures of success and collating qualitative and quantitative feedback from others, go to the supporting webpage for the book at www.datastorytellinginmarketing.com.

KEY TAKE-OUTS

1 Access proven guides, checklists, templates and shortcuts to help get you started.

2 Create your own bank of relevant archetypes, output templates and inspiring examples to provide tangible ideas for others to borrow.

3 Define and measure what successful data storytelling looks like in your world to demonstrate the effectiveness of the approach.

12

What next?

A summary of the key data storytelling actions

The 5Rs roadmap has taken you through:

---

5 key stages in the journey:

1 Plan a relevant data story.

2 Discover a robust data story.

3 Build a refined data story.

4 Create a relatable data story.

5 Execute a remarkable data story.

---

15 steps to best practice:

1 Identify the story transformation.

2 Align the story to the bigger picture.

3 Focus on a killer question.

4 Access a range of high-quality data sources.

5 Question the data observations.

6 Draw out meaningful insight.

7 Distil insights into points of view.

8 Stress-test your recommendation.

9 Weave together into a compelling narrative.

10 Integrate human experience and real-world examples.

11 Add the personal touch.

12 Keep the momentum going.

13 Optimize existing data story outputs.

14 Curate a range of digestible micro-content.

15 Incorporate interactive techniques into the story delivery.

---

30 recommended tasks:

1 Do your homework on the audience.

2 Reflect on typical transformation examples.

3 Identify the relevant source of value.

4 Define the problem statement.

5 Go beyond the objective.

6 Hypothesize the answer.

7 Find out what data sources are available.

8 Speak to an expert or the data owner.

9 Check the findings are valid.

10 Build confidence in your interpretation.

11 Dig deeper into the data.

12 Interrogate the data for the 'So what?'

13 Recode to three to five points of view.

14 Go back and answer the killer question.

15 Review desirability against feasibility.

16 Assess commercial viability.

17 Follow a storytelling framework.

18 Ruthlessly edit for clarity.

19 Utilize qualitative data.

20 Incorporate into a story hook.

21 Pick a perspective.

22 Tailor specific outputs.

23 Craft your points of view into story peaks.

24 Finish on a high point.

25 Rethink your data visualization.

26 Create powerful commentary.

27 Think digital and physical.

28 Tap into existing channels.

29 Leave space in your agenda.

30 Spark a conversation.

Words of advice

Take what you need from the 5Rs data storytelling roadmap. Don't feel the need to complete all 30 tasks for every data story. Use it as encouragement to push outside your comfort zone and experiment with new ideas.

And don't wait for the perfect project with the perfect stakeholder and the perfect data to come along before you start putting it into practice. You'll be waiting a long time!

Finding further inspiration

Finding inspiration for data storytelling can come from various sources and provide you with plenty of hints and tips you can adopt or adapt into your own work. As well as sourcing examples, remember to critically analyse and deconstruct why the data story resonates with you, and share this with others. Inspiration can come from a diverse range of sources and below are suggestions for where to start looking:

- Follow data-driven journalism websites like *The Guardian*'s Datablog, FiveThirtyEight, or the *New York Times*' The Upshot.
- Read books on data visualization and storytelling.
- Explore infographic websites such as Visual.ly or Information is Beautiful, where they showcase different examples to help spark your own creativity.
- Engage with the data storytelling community on social media platforms by following hashtags such as #dataviz or #datastorytelling to discover new trends and innovative approaches.
- Draw inspiration from art, design, photography, museum curation and interactive experiences – ask yourself what you can bring into your world.
- Study case studies of successful data storytelling projects.
- Ask for training to ensure you have a toolkit to draw on for your different data storytelling projects.

To access public domain examples, our recommended reading lists and 'who's who' to follow on social media, go to the supporting webpage for the book at www.datastorytellinginmarketing.com.

A final word

Thank you for embracing the topic of data storytelling and for allowing me to take you on this journey. I hope you have found this book an insightful and helpful guide to developing great data stories.

Whether you are looking to use the learnings from this book to tap into new ideas to support existing capabilities, or you aspire to become a world-class data storytelling champion, I wish you good luck in your data storytelling endeavours.

To gain access to more content please go to www.datastory tellinginmarketing.com or for regular inspiration follow our company page on LinkedIn at www.linkedin.com/company/insight-narrator-ltd and sign up for the newsletter.

Finally, as you put the roadmap into practice, I would love for you to share your own case study examples. You can share your thoughts and access additional content by going to www.datastorytellinginmarketing. com and joining our champions' community.

Until then…

INDEX

Note: page numbers in italic indicate figures

A/B testing 209, 231
account-based marketing 181–82
accountability 104, 213, 217, 218, 224, 225
acquisition goals 105
action items (workshops) 244
action objective questions 110
actionable insights 5–6, 54–55, 78, 111, 257
active listening tasks 217
Acxiom 4
ad hoc data stories 195, 197
advertising 52–53, 114–15, 124, 149, 157
aggregators 4
agility (always on apos marketing) 29, 45,
    53–54, 57, 63, 241, 245
alliance building 226
alphabetical information 204
Amazon 46, 123
anchoring bias 126
annotations 206, 249
anxious data storytelling consumers 12–13
archive data 229
area charts 204
Art of Persuasion (Aristotle) 22–27
artificial intelligence (AI) 31–36
generative 7, 180
attention (concentration) spans 173, 185,
    215
    see also memory (recall)
audience 99–100, 169–70, 179, 180–81
    motivation of 102
    primary 27, 103
    understanding of material 217, 257
    see also customers
audio data 36, 184, 196, 250, 254
auditory learners 201
augmented reality 36
authenticity 96, 154, 175
automation 7, 75, 144
automotive sector 194–97
averages 132, 183

bad news 147–48
bar charts 170, 205

beauty market 43, 48
'begin with end in mind' 228–29
beginnings (storyboards) 188–89
benchmarking 110, 182, 252
bespoke templates 255–56
bias 38, 66, 98, 113, 125–26, 171, 172, 183
biochemical responses 174
board reports 143, 144, 194–95, 196
booklets 211
BookTok 46
brainstorming 95, 114, 195, 235, 243
Brand Blog, The 48
brand management 30
brand perception 95, 194
B2B market 55, 178, 179, 182, 256
budgets 44, 48–49, 63, 101, 106, 114–15
bullet points 158, 194, 205, 250, 251
business schools 72–73, 230
business understanding 229
    see also context; strategy
business value 105–06
buy-in (engagement) 47–54, 101, 121,
    143–44, 213, 257

calls to action 23, 108, 187, 252
campaign data 4–5, 44
Campaign for Real Beauty 48
Canva 202
case studies 146, 261, 262
category information 204–05
CeraVe 43
challenging status quo 58–59, 78–79
champions 66, 223–39, 245
change, resistance to 102
charity sector xxi, 44
charts 204–05
bar charts 170
Chat GPT 33
checklists 206, 227, 248–49, 256
chief executive officers (CEOS) 50–51, 181
chief financial officers (CFOs) 50–52
'choose your own adventure' endings 186
Christmas advertising 53

Looking for another book?

Explore our award-winning
books from global business
experts in Marketing and Sales

Scan the code to browse

www.koganpage.com/marketing